GOOD HOUSEKEEPING

SLIM & FIT FAMILY COOK BOOK

GOOD HOUSEKEEPING

SLIM & FIT
FAMILY COOK BOOK

GOOD HOUSEKEEPING INSTITUTE

Consultant Nutritionist
JENNY SALMON

EBURY PRESS
London

Published by Ebury Press
National Magazine House
72 Broadwick Street
London W1V 2BP

First impression 1982

ISBN 0 85223 242 X (hardback)
ISBN 0 85223 255 1 (paperback)

Photography by Christine Hanscomb
Illustrations by Ken Laidlaw
and Sheila Tizzard
Designed by Jim Bunker

The publishers would like to thank Divertimenti
for their help in providing props for photography,
and The Health Education Council and
the City Gym for permission to reproduce
the exercise schedule.

Typeset by Advanced Filmsetters (Glasgow) Limited
Printed and bound by New Interlitho s.p.a., Milan

Contents

Conversion to Metric Measurements

The metric measures in this book are based on a 25-g unit instead of the ounce (28.35 g). Slight adjustments to this basic conversion standard were necessary in some recipes to achieve satisfactory cooking results.

If you want to convert your own recipes from imperial to metric, we suggest you use the same 25-g unit, and use 600 ml in place of 1 pint, with the British Standard 5-ml and 15-ml spoons replacing the old variable tea-spoons and tablespoons. These adaptations will sometimes give a slightly smaller recipe quantity and may require a shorter cooking time.

Note Sets of British Standard metric measuring spoons are available in the following sizes —
2.5 ml, 5 ml, 10 ml and 15 ml.

When measuring milk it is more convenient to use the exact conversion of 568 ml (1 pint).

For more general reference, the following tables will be helpful.

METRIC CONVERSION SCALE

| | LIQUID | | | SOLID | |
Imperial	*Exact conversion*	*Recommended ml*	Imperial	*Exact conversion*	*Recommended g*
¼ pint	142 ml	150 ml	1 oz	28.35 g	25 g
½ pint	284 ml	300 ml	2 oz	56.7 g	50 g
1 pint	568 ml	600 ml	4 oz	113.4 g	100 g
1½ pints	851 ml	900 ml	8 oz	226.8 g	225 g
1¾ pints	992 ml	1 litre	12 oz	340.2 g	350 g
			14 oz	397.0 g	400 g
			16 oz (1 lb)	453.6 g	450 g

For quantities of 1¾ pints and over, litres and fractions of a litre have been used.

1 kilogram (kg) equals 2.2 lb.

Note Follow either the metric or imperial measures for the recipes in this book as they are not interchangeable.

OVEN TEMPERATURE CHART

°C	°F	*Gas mark*	°C	°F	*Gas mark*
110	225	¼	190	375	5
130	250	½	200	400	6
140	275	1	220	425	7
150	300	2	230	450	8
170	325	3	240	475	9
180	350	4			

Foreword

Eating habits are much talked about these days and it's easy to become confused by the widely varying advice provided by the experts. Sometimes it seems that what one person says is good for us one day, another proclaims as bad the next! The *Good Housekeeping Slim & Fit Family Cook Book* provides practical, sensible advice on nutrition and outlines a realistic eating plan for the whole family.

The advice given in this book reflects current thinking that we would all be a bit healthier if we ate less fat, more dietary fibre and fewer calories, and took a little more exercise. However, this is not a 'slimming' book or a 'health food' book; it simply emphasises the importance of maintaining a healthy, balanced diet.

The recipes have been specially selected to make cooking nutritious, satisfying dishes easy, and to provide lots of ideas for family meals and for entertaining. To help you keep an eye on how much fat and fibre, or how many calories, you're eating, each recipe has symbols giving an indication as to the contents of one . portion of the made-up dishes (see below). These and the calorie (kJ) counts are only approximate but they will give you an idea of how much fat, fibre and energy one recipe contains compared with another. Remember that made-up dishes are not the only source of dietary fibre, and you can always supplement a meal with a slice of wholemeal bread or extra vegetables if you prefer not to select a high-fibre recipe.

All the recipes have been double-tested in the Good Housekeeping Institute so you can be sure of success. If you have any queries, write to

Good Housekeeping Institute
National Magazine House
72 Broadwick Street
London W1V 2BP

enclosing a stamped, addressed envelope for a personal reply.

FAT		FIBRE	
Low (0–4 g)	□	Low (0–3 g)	△
Medium (5–11 g)	▨	Medium (4–9 g)	△△
High (over 11 g)	■	High (over 9 g)	△△△

FAMILY NUTRITION

Introduction

Eating healthily is fun. Choosing foods to keep your family as fit as possible isn't difficult and healthy meals taste delicious.

All these statements are, or should be, true. They can be true for you if you take a little time to think about the food you and your family eat, and to think positively about food and health.

Most people know that food plays an important part in determining their health, but all too often these thoughts are pushed into the background in the hurly-burly of daily meal preparation. There never seems to be enough time these days, so it's not surprising that speed of preparation, convenience and keeping the whole family happy become the major considerations when deciding what to prepare for family meals.

It's precisely because you don't have to think about the old favourites that the habits of a lifetime tend to go on and on. Making changes requires thought and effort — even deciding to drive a different way into work means looking at a map, working out the new route and thinking about where you're going as you drive along.

So, if you decide that your family's diet could do with some improvement, the changes have to be worked out and implemented. You do have to give it some thought and make a little effort. The information and recipes in this book will make it easier and very soon the new ways of eating you adopt will become habits, needing very little or no effort. It is foolish to suggest that changing old habits is easy — it isn't — but nor is it that difficult and the results are worth it. The best 'present' you can give your children, and grandchildren, is an appreciation of what healthy food is all about, not by talking about it, but by example in everyday eating. Then they won't have to think about changing their eating habits at the age of 20, 30 or 50 and they'll have had the benefit of good food all their lives.

JUST HOW IMPORTANT IS FOOD?

Is it really worth thinking about the kind of food you eat? Does it have that much effect on health and well-being?

If you think about what happens when someone *stops* eating, the effects this has on weight, then eyesight, skin and general health make it very obvious that food is important. We expect a 3-kg (6½-lb) baby to grow into a 75-kg (12-stone) man. All that extra bone, muscle, skin and blood is derived from food. Maybe these two examples are, respectively, extreme and obvious, but they do make the point that getting enough food is important.

What about the type of food we eat? We've all seen pictures of young children in Africa who are blind because they don't get enough vitamin A. Some time ago, scurvy among sailors was very common because they had no fresh fruits and vegetables and so didn't eat any vitamin C. There are other examples which illustrate that the kind of food we eat is as important as the amount.

Not so long ago in this country, the main aim was for people simply to eat enough food to prevent them feeling hungry. Now the pendulum has swung — some would say too far — and practically every disease and disorder, from constipation and acne to coronary heart disease and appendicitis, is attributed to faulty diet. The people who blame diet for almost every conceivable complaint are probably going a bit too far but who should we believe?

It is not a bit surprising that some people are so fed up with the arguments about butter and margarine, bran and sugar that they've simply given up. Their view is that it's not worth changing their diets until the so-called 'experts' agree about what should be done. Even though that attitude is entirely understandable, it's a pity it exists because there is a great deal we do know to be true.

Most people can do something positive about eating more healthily without becoming cranky or neurotic about it.

WHAT SHOULD WE EXPECT FROM A GOOD DIET?

Eating well will enable each of us to grow as we should. It will also help us to get over infections as quickly as possible, but it won't put an end to the common cold or stop influenza from striking.

Almost certainly, smoking and lack of exercise are at least as important as food in affecting health, but that is no reason to dismiss food as unimportant. It helps to get things into perspective. Eating well may help to prevent several of today's disorders like heart disease and some cancers. It will certainly prevent deficiency diseases like scurvy and night blindness, and it will keep you at the right weight.

However, because we don't know all the answers yet, we can't give definitive advice for all time. The best we can do is to help people understand the present beliefs and to help them incorporate current recommendations into everyday eating. It's quite possible that future research will result in some of those recommendations changing a little.

Above all, meals should be a pleasure. They should be based on normal, everyday foods which are well chosen and well cooked. Healthy eating doesn't demand that you scour the countryside looking for hazelnut trees. Nor does it require you to increase your food budget. Indeed, it is quite likely that many people will save money by changing to a healthier diet.

Changing for the better

AREN'T WE ALL WELL FED NOW?

Newspaper, magazine and radio features so often give advice about what we should and should not eat that it's easy to gain the impression that we are all eating ourselves into early graves. This clearly isn't so. If we measure the healthiness of diet purely in terms of lifespan it seems there's not much to worry about—never before have the elderly made up such a large proportion of the population in this country. Just 100 years ago, only 6 babies in 10 reached adulthood and life expectation was, at best, 50. The main causes of ill-health were tuberculosis and infections like whooping cough, scarlet fever and diphtheria. Today the infant mortality rate is much reduced and most of the infectious diseases have been virtually eradicated.

These improvements have been brought about by a mixture of better housing, cleaner air, better sanitation, and more and better food. Medicine, in the form of surgery and other cures, has made considerable strides, but the majority of improvements in health have come through prevention. And it seems likely that prevention is the key to even better health in the future.

In the field of nutrition, vitamin deficiency diseases are almost unheard of these days and food supplies in this country are plentiful and varied. Nearly all children reach the height they should and, although cases of malnutrition do exist, they are very rare. So much has improved.

However, many people—both men and women—still die or become disabled through diseases like coronary thrombosis, cancer and stroke before they are 50. Many more are overweight which often leads to middle-age diabetes and makes arthritis even more painful. Although smoking is a major cause of some disorders, diet is important too.

We all have the choice to eat healthily or unhealthily. The difference between a good and a not-so-good diet may not sound dramatic. It isn't a question of cutting out any food for all time. It's simply a matter of understanding what needs changing and making relatively small adjustments so that the *balance* of different foods is altered; you eat more of some things, less of others.

Even a perfect diet can't overcome a life-time of inactivity and smoking, of wearing ill-fitting shoes or not going to the dentist regularly, but it can do a great deal to help.

SO WHAT NEEDS CHANGING?

Let's make it clear that some people are already eating a very good diet. For them, nothing needs changing. For the rest—probably the majority of us—we should be eating less sugar, less fat of all kinds, more dietary fibre, more starch, and fewer calories. Cutting sugar would help reduce the number of bad teeth which have to be extracted or filled each year. Taking these measures as a whole, they would correct or prevent obesity, some intestinal disorders like constipation, and could help in the fight against heart disease and some cancers.

The younger you start eating healthily the better, but it's never too late (well, almost never) to exchange bad habits for good. Admittedly, if you've lived for 70 years and smoked for 60 of them, been 3 stone over-weight for your entire adult life and have a perfect set of teeth despite a daily con-sumption of toffees, one can only look on in envy and amazement! Carry on doing what you've always done, enjoy it and look down in pity on the rest of us. Most people aren't so lucky!

If you do decide to make some changes to the family meals, it's essential that you finish up serving food that people want to eat. You may even have to make some compro-mises between healthy food and enjoyment. There's no point in living to the age of 95 because you always ate what did you good but hated every meal.

Changing your own eating habits may not be so difficult if you are convinced that such changes will benefit you. Regrettably, the same is not always true for younger members of the family. Many of today's health prob-lems take years—decades—to develop and you can't see what's going on inside the body to monitor their progress. For example, we can't see or feel the gradual hardening of the arteries so we are unaware of what's happen-ing; there is no visible reason to change the diet. Even tooth decay is not a very immediate consequence of excess sugar eat-ing. Children are not impressed with the prospect of being healthier in middle-age if they eat certain things now. When you're 5 or 15 years old, it's impossible to imagine ever reaching the age of 45. Much less does the 15-year-old care whether it's a healthy or decrepit middle-age that lies in store.

For young people, and maybe husbands too, the answer is to introduce change slowly and without talking about it. It's certainly a mistake to try to persuade people to eat food because it's 'healthy' and 'good for them'.

Understanding our needs

WHAT IS A 'GOOD' DIET?

Most definitions of a 'good' diet sound trite in the extreme—'Foods that provide enough energy and all nutrients for optimal health'. That gets us nowhere. The argument against a more precise definition is that people vary so much that what may be a 'good' diet for one person may not be for another. It's not unknown for one person to need twice as much vitamin C (or other nutrient) as another, apparently similar, person.

Advice about a better diet is often given in terms of 'eat less of X, Y and Z, eat more of A and B'. But less than what, more than what? Some people are already eating what they should and they don't need to change. If you do need to change, how do you know by how much?

WHAT NUTRIENTS DO WE NEED?

A little later in this chapter we'll try to put some figures on various nutrients so that you can calculate just how well your diet measures up to current recommendations, but before that, we need to consider the nutrients we all need.

We need to eat specific amounts of dozens of nutrients—20 amino acids make up proteins, there are 13 vitamins and a couple of dozen minerals—as well as fats, carbohydrates (sugars and starches), dietary fibre and water.

It's obvious that children need the nutrients that make blood, bone, skin, kidneys, etc, because they are growing. However, even when growth in height stops, the individual cells which make up the different organs in the body are constantly dying and being replaced by new cells. This process goes on in adults and children, so everyone needs the same kinds of nutrients throughout life. The difficult question to answer is how much?

The Department of Health and Social Security in this country produces a list of Recommended Daily Amounts detailing energy, protein, 2 minerals (calcium and iron) and 6 of the 13 vitamins the authorities think we should eat each day. The quantities recommended are enough even for people with high needs. The amount of energy suggested is the average for each age group—some people will need less, some more, than the suggested figure to maintain their body weight.

What about all the other nutrients, the remaining 7 vitamins and at least a dozen minerals and trace elements we need to keep healthy? These aren't detailed because, it's argued, if people eat foods to give enough of the nutrients that *are* listed they'll also be getting enough of those that aren't. Which is a relief, because no one would want to sit down and calculate the amounts of four dozen nutrients eaten, even for just one day!

Every year the National Food Survey Committee monitors all the food some 7000 families eat in a week. They calculate how nutritionally adequate the diets are and compare the results with the recommended nutritional needs. Each year the results show that, on average, the normal diet in this country supplies more than enough of almost all nutrients and energy. Some children may not be eating enough vitamin D, but as long as these children get out in the sunshine they can make their own vitamin D. So, by and large, everything looks fine and you might interpret the results as a signal to 'carry on as usual'.

The problem is that there are no recommendations about the amounts of fat, sugar or dietary fibre we should be eating, and the National Food Survey doesn't monitor these components. Nor are there any recommendations about the amount of folic acid we ought to eat. Folic acid is one of the 8 vitamins which make up the B group and is needed for the proper formation of red blood cells. There is some evidence that pregnant women in particular may not be eating enough folic acid. We can see that many children have bad teeth, suggesting that they eat too much sugar, and there is a suspicion that the amount of fat in the diet is too high.

So although many nutrients seem to be present in the diet in sufficient amounts, a few may be marginal and some over-represented. We'll look at these now.

FAT supplies us with energy, and not long ago we thought that was its only function, but it is actually much more complex. Fats are made up of mixtures of fatty acids which may be 'saturated', 'monounsaturated' or 'polyunsaturated'. Saturated fatty acids are found mainly in meat fat, cheese, lard, cream, palm oil and cooking oil. Monounsaturated fatty acids are the main components of olive oil but are also found in many other foods. Polyunsaturated fatty acids are found in vegetable oils, like sunflower, safflower and corn oil, and in margarines made from them. The fats in oily fish and poultry are less saturated than other animal fats. Quite apart from the energy these supply, every cell in the body needs a tiny amount of polyunsaturated fatty acid to help make the structure of the cell wall. Some of the fatty acids are converted to prostaglandins in the body—substances which act on many systems to keep them functioning properly.

The amount of fat we need to supply these needs is about 4 g per day—the equivalent of a few teaspoons of corn oil or fish oil. In other words, not much. The average actual intake is over 100 g a day—all of which provides us with energy.

What about the different kinds of fatty acids? A great deal has been written about fats and heart disease and the rôle of different kinds of fatty acids. Despite all the observations, diet manipulations and new foods 'rich in polyunsaturates', we still don't know the exact rôle of the different fatty acids in causing heart disease—if any. We do know that people with a lot of cholesterol (a fatty substance) in their blood are more likely than others to have a heart attack. We also know that eating more polyunsaturated fats reduces blood cholesterol while saturated fats increase it. However, there is no real proof that lowering blood cholesterol level by changing the diet actually prevents heart attacks. Almost certainly, heredity (which you can't change) and smoking and inactivity (which you can) are more important factors than fat or diet. So, as far as heart disease is concerned, the best thing is to eat as little fat as possible. Take some from fish and, for the rest, eat butter or margarine. The younger a person is when he starts eating a low fat diet, the better.

One thing we know for certain about fat in food is that it contains lots of energy. (Energy is usually measured in kilocalories—'kcals'—but can also be measured as kilojoules—'kJ'. Kilocalories are more normally referred to as Calories. There are about 4 kJ to every kcal.) Every gram of fat—about the amount you'd get on a salt spoon (about a fifth of a level teaspoon)—contains 9 kcals or 37 kJ. The same amount of sugar, protein, starch or even alcohol doesn't contain that much energy. Therefore, all foods which contain a high proportion of fat also contain a large amount of energy. So fat intake is probably the most important factor determining a person's weight. Altogether there is a strong case for looking at the amount of fat you eat and, probably, cutting it down no matter what kind of fat it is.

SUGAR, like fat, helps to supply energy but its other 'claim to fame' is that it rots children's teeth.

There are different kinds of sugars—sucrose or table sugar is the most common by far. Then there's lactose (the sugar in milk), fructose (found in fruits) and glucose (also found in fruits). Of all these, sucrose is the most likely to cause tooth decay. They all contain about 3.75 kcals (16 kJ) per gram. Don't imagine that glucose is that much better for you than sucrose. Because it is less sweet you may be tempted to use more glucose than sucrose to get the same sweet taste—and that means you'll be getting more energy!

Despite the fact that one third of people in this country over the age of 16 have lost all their natural teeth, tooth decay and dental disease are not inevitable. Most teeth are lost by a combination of too many sticky sweets and too little use of the toothbrush. Perhaps surprisingly, it isn't so much the total amount of sucrose that is the critical factor in tooth decay. Rather it's the number of times in a day a person eats sucrose and the time the sugar stays in contact with the teeth. The more often sugar is eaten and the more it adheres to the tooth and gum surfaces, the more likely it is that tooth decay will become a problem.

Bacteria of various kinds live in the mouth. They stick to the teeth and gums in a substance called plaque. They have the capacity to grow and multiply with amazing speed. Each bacterial cell can grow and divide into two every half hour, providing it has enough of the right kind of food.

To mouth bacteria, sucrose is food. So, as long as there is sucrose around, they are active and one of their waste products is acid. This is eliminated from the bacterial cell and becomes trapped in the sticky plaque where it 'eats' into tooth enamel—and beyond.

If everyone cleaned their teeth after every bout of sweet-eating, the plaque, bacteria, acid and sugar would be removed and there would be no decay. That is a counsel of perfection and unlikely to happen. The next best thing is to cut down on the number of times sugar is eaten and to try to make the form of the sugar as liquid and 'unsticky' as possible. Two puddings a day are preferable to sweets every half hour.

If no toothbrush is to hand after a meal, nuts and a tiny piece of cheese are better than an apple. The nuts and cheese don't prevent acid forming but they do neutralise it and help prevent erosion of tooth enamel.

Apart from tooth decay, all sugars supply energy. Foods rich in sugar often contain lots of fat too which means lots of calories, and not much in the way of vitamins and minerals.

STARCHES, like sugars, are very often considered 'bad' nutrients because they make people fat. This simply isn't true. Starches don't cause tooth decay and they are not as high in calories as fat or alcohol. More importantly, foods containing a large amount of starch are nearly always sources of several minerals and vitamins. For example, potatoes, bread and pasta all have a lot of starch but they also have a host of other nutrients and not too many calories. They also have almost no fat.

DIETARY FIBRE is often found, in reasonable amounts, in starchy foods. Next to the topic of fats and heart disease, dietary fibre must rate top of the 1980s medicine league of popular talking points. Of course, 'roughage' has been around as long as food itself and people even recognised it as a component of some foods. In the space of 10 years, 'roughage' has come out of the dark. It has a new name, a new image and has generally achieved respectability alongside all the other nutrients. Perhaps predictably, the claims made for the health-giving proper-

ties of dietary fibre have been over-stated by some people and are pushing scientific niceties a bit too far. There's no doubt though that an adequate intake of dietary fibre does prevent some disorders.

Dietary fibre is not one substance as sucrose is. It's a mixture of many. Each of the components has a structure and properties of its own. Dietary fibre is not digested by the gut enzymes that digest proteins, fats and carbohydrates, but that doesn't mean it is an inert lump which moves along the digestive tract. Many of the benefits attributed to dietary fibre stem from its 'bulking' effect. There's no doubt that it's much easier for the muscular walls of the intestines to move a large mass than a small one, and dietary fibre does prevent or cure almost all cases of constipation.

Constipation itself may not sound very dangerous, but it does bother a great many people in this country. They often treat themselves with laxatives and liquid paraffin. These are effective to begin with, but people need ever-increasing doses to get the same effect. Such medicines can cause problems for the elderly, in particular. If they forget whether they've taken their daily dose and take another one, it may cause diarrhoea. This means that minerals like potassium are lost from the body with consequent mental confusion and muscular weakness. Taking an overdose of natural dietary fibre is much less likely.

If a person is constipated, clearly the contents of the lower bowel stay in the body for a long time. There is some evidence that the bacteria which naturally live in the bowel have time to act on some of the waste components and change them into cancer-producing chemicals. This is by no means proved yet but seems to be worth considering and making sure that the diet contains enough fibre.

Whether all the benefits attributed to a high-fibre diet are true will be shown when more research has been done. Among these are the prevention of gall stones, appendicitis, hiatus hernia, diverticulitis, haemorrhoids, varicose veins, obesity and, surprise, heart disease. Most people find a high-fibre diet more satisfying so it could help to control body weight.

Dietary fibre components are found in fruits, vegetables and wholemeal cereals like bread. The different components are found in different proportions in these foods, so it makes sense to eat cereals and vegetables in reasonable quantities.

VITAMIN C Another 'popular' nutrient and one on which a good deal of research has been conducted is vitamin C. Like fats and dietary fibre, it has generated its own arguments. It's well known that this vitamin prevents scurvy. It would not be surprising if you didn't recognise a case if you came face to face with it in the street—the disease is virtually unknown in this country—but basically its symptoms are receding and bleeding gums, loose teeth and tiny haemorrhages in the skin. Wounds like broken bones and skin cuts fail to heal as quickly as they should.

Vitamin C is involved in the formation of a substance which cements adjacent body cells to each other. If we don't eat enough vitamin C the cement breaks down and insufficient new cement is formed. That explains why tiny blood vessels leak and why wounds don't heal well.

A daily 30 mg of vitamin C—the amount in one small orange—is all that anyone needs to do the cementing job. But—and herein lies the controversy—it could be that vitamin C has the potential to do more than just ward off scurvy. If we took 60–100 mg a day it would be enough to do other things as well. Among the 'other' functions of vitamin C are reducing the amount of cholesterol in the body and relieving one of the many kinds of depression (people who develop scurvy often become very depressed and lethargic before any of the other more obvious symptoms appear).

As far as anyone can tell, most people eat 30 mg vitamin C a day, but the actual intake depends very much on the amount of fruit eaten and the way vegetables are cooked. It is all too easy to boil green vegetables and potatoes so that all their vitamin C is lost. Few people, however, eat as much as 60 mg a day. It certainly won't do any harm to eat the larger amount and it may do some good What it won't do is prevent you getting a cold!

FOLIC ACID is one of the eight B group vitamins which takes part in the formation of red blood cells and so prevents a kind of anaemia. Like vitamin C, it occurs in green vegetables, but also in liver and wholemeal cereals. It is also easily dissolved out of vegetables into cooking water. There is some evidence that pregnant women don't always get enough folic acid but it would do no harm if everyone ate more green vegetables to be sure they are getting enough of this vitamin.

VITAMIN D is essential for the absorption of calcium and for its deposition in bones and teeth. The vitamin can be made in the skin so as long as enough ultra violet light (from sunlight) falls on the skin no one need eat the nutrient. Some children, especially in inner city areas, do not play out of doors and their diets don't contain any of the few vitamin D rich foods. As a result rickets is re-appearing among some young children. Foods rich in the vitamin are liver, margarine, fish liver oils and, to a lesser extent, butter, eggs and cheese.

ALCOHOL, in excess, can be dangerous for the liver, as is well known, but if alcohol begins to replace more nutritious foods a general malnutrition occurs. Recent research suggests that alcohol should not be taken except very occasionally during pregnancy to protect the unborn child.

But all is not gloom on the alcohol front. It seems that one or two 'shorts' or equivalent a day can be beneficial to health, quite apart from making life in general more pleasant.

The energy in one or two drinks won't make anyone hugely fat, but beer drinkers need to realise that one single pint gives them 200 kcal (800 kJ).

Cutting a body down to size

A major and very obvious problem deriving from both diet and lifestyle is obesity. All overweight is caused by consuming more food (and drink), i.e. more energy, than the body can use. The only way to treat it is to change the energy balance and to eat fewer calories than are needed so the body turns to its fat stores to make up the difference. This is best done by decreasing the amount of energy consumed and by increasing the amount of energy you use, for example by taking more exercise.

HOW MUCH ENERGY DO WE NEED?

The answer depends on the individual. We all need some energy from food, not only to do obviously active things like walking, making beds and running occasionally, but also just to stay alive. A surprisingly large amount of energy is used in breathing, keeping blood flowing around the body, making enzymes to digest food and keeping the amount of water in the body constant. These basic processes which go on 24 hours a day can account for anything from 1400 kcals (6000 kJ) to 2500 kcals (10,000 kJ) each day, depending on the individual person. So not only is the amount of energy large but it is very variable from person to person.

On top of these requirements, the amount of energy we need for physical activity is, of course, immensely variable. It is not unusual for an office worker who goes to work by car and who watches television most evenings to need only a few hundred kcals on top of the 'basic' requirement. On the other hand, an actively training athlete may well need a total energy intake of 4000–5000 kcals (17,000–21,000 kJ) a day if he is not to lose weight.

As an average, women need about 2100 kcals (8700 kJ) each day to maintain their ideal weight. For men the equivalent figure is about 2700 kcals (11,300 kJ).

One thing is certain, if you are too fat you are eating more energy than you need and you should eat less—about 1200 kcals (5000 kJ) for women, 1500 kcals (6200 kJ) for men and children. You may not be eating more than your friend, but that is irrelevant. You are eating more than you are using.

WHERE IS THE ENERGY IN FOOD?

Nutrients like protein, fat and vitamin C can be extracted from foods and drinks and you can actually see them. It's impossible to extract energy and look at that. The energy in foods is contained in proteins, fats, starches, sugars and alcohol in much the same way as energy is a part of the structure of coal. The energy in foods is released and made available within the body when the molecules of proteins, etc, are changed by a series of reactions into smaller compounds—ultimately to carbon dioxide, water and urea.

Even protein, which is taken from food to form part of the body structure (tissue), is eventually removed from the tissue and used as a source of energy. So all food protein can be considered to contribute to the total energy intake. It's obvious therefore that it's quite wrong to say that protein-rich foods, such as meat, are 'not fattening': they contain energy just as all other foods do and whether a person gets fat or thin depends not on individual foods but on the energy content of the total diet.

When used by the body, each gram of protein gives 4 kcals (17 kJ), a gram of fat gives 9 kcals (37 kJ), a gram of alcohol 7 kcals

(29 kJ), and each gram of carbohydrate supplies 3.75 kcals (16 kJ).

WHY DO WE GET FAT WHEN WE EAT TOO MUCH ENERGY?

Unfortunately, most of us can't get rid of an excess of energy if we eat too much. We have no built-in waste disposal unit for it. The few fortunate people who can eat huge amounts and still not put on weight do have such a system—it seems to be in the small patches of brown fat cells in the body. They just 'burn off' the excess.

For the majority of us, however, once energy is inside the body it stays there until it's used. What happens is that the molecules of protein, fat, carbohydrate and alcohol which are not needed immediately are converted by a series of reactions to form body fat, and they take their energy with them and store it until it is needed.

Eating 3500 kcals (14,500 kJ) more than the body needs means that 500 g (1 lb) of body fat is formed. It doesn't make much difference whether the extra energy comes from proteins, fats, carbohydrates or alcohol, it will all be stored in the same way.

WHAT KIND OF SLIMMING DIET?

The only slimming diet which works is an energy-reduced one. Somehow you must eat fewer calories than the body needs so that the extra energy needed is supplied by body fat and fat is removed. It doesn't matter whether the slimming diet is called low fat, low carbohydrate, high protein, egg and spinach or biscuits and milk—if it means you eat fewer calories, it will work. If it doesn't reduce your energy intake, your body won't need to use its energy stores, and you won't lose any weight.

Most people find that the best method of losing weight is to count calories and to eat the foods they like within the allotted energy total for the day. Eating the kinds of foods shown on page 20 ensures you stay healthy as you slim.

CAN EXERCISE HELP?

If you don't like exerting yourself you will cling like a limpet to the fact that you have to walk from London to Brighton to lose just 500 g (1 lb) of fat. Exercise is useful, in conjunction with eating less food, because it helps to control the amount of food you actually want to eat. It seems that the appetite control mechanism in the brain which should tell us when we feel hungry and when we feel full, works a great deal better if we take a little regular exercise, preferably soon after eating. That doesn't mean jumping into the swimming pool after a seven-course meal. It does mean a gentle walk, and some vigorous exercise at least three times a week. Quite apart from helping to control food intake and working off a little energy, regular exercise makes the heart work harder and so is good for general health.

We have included a schedule of exercises (see page 140) which, if done regularly could help in reducing weight. The exercises have been specially chosen to improve the general fitness of the whole family and will help build up stamina, strength and mobility, as well as burn up some of that excess energy.

HOW FAST SHOULD YOU LOSE WEIGHT?

Once some people have made up their minds to lose weight, they expect instant results. It is of no consequence to them that it took 3500 kcals (14,500 kJ) over and above the body's needs to add a mere pound in the first place. They expect to lose half a stone in the first 3 days. But even starvation would result in only about 3 kg (6 lb) of fat being lost in a week. There may be some loss of body water at the same time which makes results seem more impressive, but that water will be replaced the following week.

If you lose more than about 1 kg (2 lb) of *fat* a week, a fair proportion of that extra will be body muscle, not fat. And that's not the object of the exercise at all. Crash diets do no harm for a few days to get the bathroom scales moving in the right direction, but they are not sensible for longer than that.

Slimming to a nice lean shape and to a good average weight (taking height and body-build into account) is the ideal for appearance and optimal health, but over-slimming and becoming obsessive about weight can be dangerous.

There's no getting away from the fact that some young people overdo it and take slimming so far that they continue to lose weight long after their 'ideal' weight has been reached. In extreme form, this is *anorexia nervosa*, a severe psychological disorder in which the person eats far too little, or actually nothing at all. Self-starvation of this kind is difficult to cure: far better to prevent it by cultivating, within the family, a healthy, non-obsessive attitude to life, food and body weight. Healthy eating should become a matter of course, and family conversation should not dwell on diets, calorie counting and 'slimming' foods.

Anorexia tends to occur in teenagers rather than adults, in women rather than men. Encouraging people to be slim and to lose weight sensibly is fine, making an issue of an overweight, sensitive teenager's size is not. Parents should be suspicious if a teenage girl appears to be eating very little, or refusing to eat anything but 'non-fattening' foods; if she has occasional 'binges', possibly followed by vomiting, while otherwise sticking to a rigid diet; if she shows great interest in food and cooking, but does not eat herself; if she does 'slimming' exercises to excess; if her periods become very irregular, or cease altogether; above all, if she is clearly very thin but denies this, and continues to make efforts to lose weight. Some, or all, of these signs indicate that the young person is becoming anorexic, and medical help should be sought immediately, however unwilling the victim is to concede that there is anything wrong.

WHAT'S THE GOOD OF BEING SLIM?

Apart from feeling and looking better, there are definite health benefits in being the correct weight. One of the major advantages is that many cases of middle-age diabetes can be prevented or cured just by slimming. Maturity onset diabetes isn't so severe that insulin injections are needed, but the diet has to be adjusted and blood and urine samples tested regularly and sometimes tablets taken. In addition, diabetics are more likely than other people to get other disorders. For the majority of sufferers, life returns to normal if they just lose weight.

In addition, the pain of arthritis and hiatus hernia are lessened and it is much easier to walk up stairs without puffing like a steam engine if you have no extra fat to carry with you. When you realise that 6 or 7 kg (1 stone) of extra body fat weighs the same as 4 large bags of flour you can understand what a strain it is. Apart from these benefits which become immediately apparent when weight is lost, there is less chance of a slim person— man or woman—suffering a heart attack.

Being slim is important to good health, but it isn't the end of healthy, balanced eating. It is possible to slim and be slim by eating a rather poor diet.

The real business of eating

Now we know the possible consequences of too much fat and too many calories, too much sugar and not enough vitamin C, folic acid and dietary fibre, how does *your* diet shape up?

EATING THE RIGHT THINGS

We'll discuss fat, calories and dietary fibre in a moment, but let's deal with all the other nutrients like protein, calcium and iron to begin with. After all, there's no point in paying attention to the 'problem' nutrients if, in doing so, you cut yourself short of something else.

The one golden rule of general healthy eating is to eat as many different foods as possible in the course of a week. By doing so, you can be sure you're eating all the vitamins, minerals and trace elements you need. You should eat as many of the following as possible:

Bread, pasta, pizza and breakfast cereals
Potatoes
Peas, broad beans and baked beans
Leafy green vegetables
Root vegetables
Citrus fruits
Other fruits
Carcass meats
Poultry
White fish
Oily fish
Cheese, milk and yogurt
Eggs

No single food is nutritionally perfect which means no food contains all the nutrients we need in the correct amounts. For example, bread contains some protein, starch, dietary

A Guide to Daily Intakes

		Fat (g)	Energy (kcals)	(kJ)
Children	age 3–4	50–60	1550	6500
	5–6	55–65	1700	7100
	7–8	65–75	1950	8200
	9–11	75–90	2200	9200
Teenage boys		90–105	2700	11300
Teenage girls		70–85	2100	8700
Men—moderately active	age 18–34	95–110	2900	12100
	35–65	90–105	2700	11300
sedentary	over 65	75–85	2200	9200
Women	age 18–55	70–80	2100	8700
	over 55	60–70	1800	7500

If you are very active you will need more energy and can therefore have more fat. If you are slimming on a 1200-kcal (5000-kJ) diet you'll only need about 40–45 g fat a day. Men trying to lose weight by eating 1500 kcals (6200 kJ) a day would take 50–60 g fat.

FAMILY NUTRITION

fibre, iron and several B group vitamins; peas have vitamin C, dietary fibre and some vitamin A and minerals as well as protein; and beef has protein, fat, iron and several B group vitamins.

The chart on page 20 gives an indication of the amounts of energy different people need each day. If most of that energy is obtained by eating most of the foods listed, enough of all nutrients will be obtained. Remember that these energy values are only a guide, you may need more or less. If you're trying to lose weight you'll certainly need less—1200 kcals (5000 kJ) for women, 1500 kcals (6200 kJ) for men and children.

You can be sure of eating enough vitamin C each day if you take a glass of orange juice, one potato and a good portion of green vegetables—not overcooked, please. Folic acid is a bit more difficult, but liver once a week is an enormous help—it really is verging on the 'wonder' food. Apart from that you'll get some from the orange juice and you'll need some dark green vegetables like spinach, broccoli and Brussels sprouts. Wholemeal bread will help too.

Now we can tackle the other problem nutrients—fat and dietary fibre.

FAT Although there are no official Recommended Daily Amounts for fat intake, many people think it would be sensible if fat provided only about 30–35 per cent of the total energy intake. A few people eat less than this now, most of us eat more. On average, fat supplies over 40 per cent of the total energy in the nation's diet. The chart shows how much fat different groups of people should aim to eat in a day. For most it's better to eat less than more.

You can see how your diet compares by writing down all the foods you eat for at least 3 days. You'll need to make a guess at the amount of each food eaten, and remember to include drinks like milk. Using the figures in the chart on page 33, work out the total fat intake for the 3 days and divide by 3 to get the daily average. Compare this with the appropriate figure on the Daily Intakes Guide, then you'll know whether you need to reduce your fat intake.

If you don't want to bother with notebooks and calculators you can get a rough idea of the fat contents of your foods by working out how many of the very fatty foods you eat in an average day. Foods which don't have to be considered because they contain almost no fat are cereals and bread, pasta, rice, skimmed milk and low fat yogurt, fruits and vegetables, cottage cheese and white fish. Sugar has no fat, but that's a different story.

Obviously fatty foods are butter, margarine, oils and mayonnaise, pretty well all fried food and fatty meat. But there are some surprises. Fat makes up half the weight of double cream, peanuts, walnuts and almonds, one third of the weight of chocolate and crisps, most cheeses, breast of lamb and whipping cream. If you regularly eat more than 5 'portions' of such fat-rich foods a day you are probably eating too much fat. And remember, some fat is hidden but it still counts.

DIETARY FIBRE At present, the average dietary fibre intake in this country is 20 g per person per day. Some people take as little as 6 g, others as much as 40 g. Again there are no official figures for the amount we should be eating and individual needs do vary considerably, but it isn't difficult to know when you are eating the correct amount for you. Something like 30 g a day would be a reasonable goal to begin with and you can make your own adjustments from there.

Most people know bran is a good source of fibre, and indeed it is, but there are many other foods which are a lot more palatable which should be included in the diet to provide different kinds of fibre. Peas, beans and baked beans are very good, so are nuts, wholemeal bread and bran-containing breakfast cereals. Weetabix and Shredded Wheat, porridge and most fruits and vegetables help too. No animal foods contain dietary fibre, so there is none in egg, milk, cream, yogurt, cheese, meat or fish.

A plan for good eating

The foods listed below form the basis of a healthy, balanced diet.

Each day
1 portion of bran-containing breakfast cereal
1 portion of lean meat, poultry, fish or eggs
2 portions of cheese, milk, or yogurt
4 portions of fruits or vegetables including 1 portion of peas, beans or baked beans and 1 of orange
1 portion of potato
4 slices of wholemeal bread
Each week
1 or preferably 2 portions of liver or kidney

These foods will provide enough of all the nutrients you should be eating, enough dietary fibre and about 1000–1200 kcals (4200–5000 kJ) per day. That is enough energy if you are trying to lose weight, but not enough if you are wanting to maintain an ideal weight. The basic foods provide a little fat, so some butter, cream, fried food and mayonnaise can be added to help make up the energy to the level you need. There's room for some sugar too, but most extra energy should come from eating more of the basic foods.

Remember that the way foods are cooked can have a dramatic effect on the amount of fat, and therefore the energy content, and the amount of vitamin C you actually consume. So always grill food rather than fry it wherever possible and don't overcook vegetables. More will be said about the effects of cooking later in this chapter (see page 31).

Get into the habit of removing all visible fat from meat before it's eaten, of removing poultry skin because that is fatty, and of eating lower fat cheeses, such as cottage and Edam.

THE TIMESCALE OF HEALTHY EATING

This plan is given for one day, but of course you don't want to eat the same foods every day. You don't even have to eat a perfectly balanced diet *every* day. As long as your diet is nutritionally good over a week you will be eating well.

Following the suggested plan will help develop the habit of healthy eating on most days, then if you eat a great deal of fatty food once a month it won't do any harm.

If you eat more nutrients, like vitamins and minerals, than the body needs in one day, the excess will be stored until the body stores are full. Then, for most nutrients, any further excess is excreted. The exceptions are vitamins A and D which go on accumulating in the body. Theoretically, they could reach dangerous levels, but this is most unlikely to happen if you're eating normal amounts of foods. It could happen if you take very large doses of tonics and vitamin pills.

When body stores are full, there is enough vitamin C to last for several weeks, and enough of all nutrients to last for at least 2 weeks, even if you fasted. So if you are short of one or two nutrients on one day, there's absolutely no reason to worry about it.

For all of us, there are occasions when life becomes so unbearable that only a couple of luscious cream puffs covered in chocolate will make amends. If you feel like that three days a year, eat nothing but cream puffs for those three days. If you are driven to that state three times a week, think again!

The healthy eating plan has room for every food you could possibly want to eat. It's the frequency of eating them which may need to be changed. But don't become a martyr to the cause; you'll drive yourself and everyone else mad.

HOW MANY MEALS A DAY?

More and more of our food is being eaten as snacks and very often individual members of the family eat on their own. The family meal is becoming much less common than it used to be. In itself, this may not be such a bad thing, although family meals are probably important for social reasons. In nutritional terms, however, the move to snacks could be very significant. The kinds of foods we should be placing more importance on are fish, *lean* meats, vegetables and pasta. It is quite difficult to eat these foods outside the formal meal context. They need a plate, knife and fork—if not an actual dining table. Many of today's snacks which are eaten in the fingers and need virtually no preparation are high in fat and sugar, and they are probably low in dietary fibre.

Of course it's possible to choose convenient foods which contain fibre—sandwiches made with wholemeal bread are one example, and fresh fruit is easy to eat. Pizzas are very nutritious and ice cream is better than most people think. But the chocolate bars, biscuits and soft drinks which make up such a large part of snack eating are not so good.

There is a major case to be made, therefore, for eating two or three formal meals, i.e. the kind which need a knife and fork, each day. Cutting the between-meals sugary snacks will also help teeth to stay healthy.

Improving eating patterns

Most people think they eat pretty healthily. Some are right, but others are deluding themselves. Now we know what a 'good' diet is, we can see how some typical daily meals rate against the criteria of healthy eating we have set by looking at the following examples.

JANET is in her early twenties and works in an office. There is no canteen so she has to buy her own lunch in a café or bring in sandwiches every day.

Janet probably needs no more than about 2000 kcals a day and so should have no more than 80 g fat. Her daily diet includes far too many fatty foods and bits and pieces which pile on the fat and energy. These foods don't provide nearly enough vitamin C or folic acid, and dietary fibre could be improved. Janet should eat only one small chocolate bar *or* three plain biscuits in the day. If between-meal snacks are essential they should be fresh fruit.

The evening meal could be improved if lots of green vegetables were added together

	Fat (g)	Dietary fibre (g)	kcals
Breakfast			
150 ml (¼ pint) milk for tea during the day	6	0	95
1 slice white toast	0	1.1	90
15 g (½ oz) butter	12	0	110
15 g (½ oz) marmalade	0	0	40
Mid-morning			
Doughnut	8	1.2	175
Lunch			
2 sausage rolls	10	0.3	290
small chocolate bar	15	0	320
Mid-afternoon			
3 biscuits	8	1.0	220
On way home			
2 chocolate biscuits	14	1.5	260
Evening			
small packet crisps	9	3.0	140
225 g (8 oz) shepherds' pie	13	2.0	260
175 g (6 oz) chips	20	5.4	450
50 g (2 oz) ice cream	4	0	80
1 round cheese sandwiches	43	2.2	630
1 glass milk	6	0	70
Total	168	17.7	3230

with baked beans. And there is no need for chips *and* the potato on the pie. The evening sandwich is very fatty and provides far too many excess calories.

Lunch is often a problem. Buying food at the corner shop may be satisfactory if the store is good, but more often than not it's white bread sandwiches or nothing. Eating in restaurants is too expensive to do every day. The best solution is to get into the habit of taking your own packed meal. Wholemeal bread rolls with salad and lean meat or cottage cheese, fresh fruit, a pot of cottage cheese, hot soup or meat stew in a thermos flask, low-fat yogurt and pitta bread filled

with salad vegetables and chopped cooked meat are all suitable. More interesting salads can be mixed from left-over vegetables and a little cooked rice, raisins and a few nuts.

PETER works as an accountant and he too has to provide his own midday meal—usually in the pub.

Peter probably needs about 3000 kcals a day so he's about right with the energy intake. Dietary fibre is good but he needs only about 100 g fat. He could cut fat intake by not eating the butter with his Ploughman's lunch. If lunch on other days of the week is taken in a restaurant he could choose

	Fat (g)	Dietary fibre (g)	kcals
Breakfast			
25 g (1 oz) cornflakes	0	3.7	90
150 ml (¼ pint) milk	5	0	80
15 g (½ oz) sugar	0	0	60
150 ml (¼ pint) milk for tea and coffee during the day	6	0	95
1 poached egg	6	0	90
1 slice bread	0	1.1	90
2 rashers bacon	18	0	210
Midday			
2 pints beer	0	0	400
Ploughman's lunch (cheese, French bread, pickle, butter)	67	3.2	900
Evening			
1 gin and tonic	0	0	90
30 ml (2 tbsp) peanuts	25	4.0	280
bowl clear soup	4	0	70
150 g (5–6 oz) stewed steak and kidney	12	0	180
30 ml (2 tbsp) beans	0	1.5	10
30 ml (2 tbsp) peas	0	4.0	30
3 medium boiled potatoes	0	3.0	240
45 ml (3 tbsp) fruit salad	0	2.0	50
30 ml (2 tbsp) whipping cream	17	0	60
1 bread roll—wholemeal	0	4.0	140
Total	160	26.5	3165

SLIM & FIT FAMILY COOK BOOK

lean meat or grilled fish and vegetables to balance the fatty Ploughman's.

It might be more sensible to drink only one pint of beer at lunch-time, especially if the food eaten at the same time is high in carbohydrate. There is evidence that alcohol makes the body secrete more insulin than usual and this reduces the blood glucose level during the afternoon. This results in a feeling of tiredness which is not conducive to a productive afternoon's work!

ANGELA is a housewife at home with her two-year-old all day. She has the evening meal with her husband.

Angela is typical of many mothers with young children. She is busy getting everyone off to school and work and doesn't find time to eat breakfast herself. At lunch-time she prepares food for her two-year-old, but doesn't bother about herself. The evening meal is fine. Her diet is probably low on energy and certainly contains insufficient dietary fibre and vitamin C. Because the diet as a whole is low in energy the fat content is about right. It would help if she ate some high-fibre breakfast cereal with a little milk or yogurt, or at least changed the bread to wholemeal.

At lunch-time, even if Angela doesn't want to spend ages cooking for herself she could have baked beans on wholemeal toast, a few fish fingers and peas, sardines on toast or some soup and a wholemeal bread roll. Other easy lunches are cottage cheese and a piece of fruit with bread, spaghetti in tomato sauce or

	Fat (g)	Dietary fibre (g)	kcals
Breakfast			
200 ml (7 fl oz) milk for tea and coffee during the day	8	0	130
1 slice white toast	0	1.1	90
15 g (½ oz) butter	12	0	110
15 g (½ oz) marmalade	0	0	40
Mid-morning			
50-g (2-oz) slice cake	6	1.0	160
Midday			
150 g (5–6 oz) leftover apple crumble	7	2.5	210
2 biscuits	9	1.0	230
Mid-afternoon			
2 biscuits	9	1.0	230
Evening			
150 g (5–6 oz) beef carbonnade	11	0	180
1 medium jacket potato	0	2	160
30 ml (2 tbsp) peas	0	4	30
45 ml (3 tbsp) red cabbage	0	1	15
50-g (2-oz) portion mousse	6	0	110
Total	68	13.6	1695

a well grilled beefburger in a bun. Corned beef, mashed potato (instant) and coleslaw makes a very quick, wholesome lunch.

Fresh fruit, dried fruit or a *few* nuts would be better than biscuits for the snacks.

Where do prepared foods fit into the healthy eating plan?

It is a fact of life that canned, dried, frozen and otherwise prepared foods make up a large part of our daily diets. By and large the plain foods—vegetables, fish and fruit juices contain what you'd expect in terms of nutrients. Today's methods of preserving foods don't destroy even the most easily lost nutrients to any great extent. Some vitamins are lost in the factory cooking or blanching processes but less is lost at home compared with shop- or market-bought equivalents because the cooking times are shorter.

But how do you know what's in foods like pizzas, soups and instant hot snack lunches? A few food producers are putting some nutrition information on their labels which makes life a great deal easier—you can see how much fat and how many calories there are in what you're eating. For the rest, you have to guess. You know that all pastry-based foods will be rich in fat and therefore energy; all chocolates, sweets, sweet biscuits and cake will have a lot of sugar, most will have a high proportion of fat, too. Most soups contain some fat and starch, but even vegetable soups don't contain much in the way of vitamins. Pizzas are nutritious, but a bit on the fatty side, and all fried food prepared in restaurants will be fatty and high in energy.

Some information about the ingredients of convenience foods can be gleaned from the label—the constituents have to be listed in descending order of weight. Canned pasta, dried pasta and baked beans are very low fat

foods, and contain many nutrients. Milk shakes are basically sweetened milk so they will contain quite a lot of fat, but many other nutrients too.

Many of the more usual prepared foods are included in the chart on pages 33–41.

Special needs and eating patterns

The healthy eating plan we have outlined assumes that everyone will want to eat pretty well all the foods available in this country. But some, for one reason or another, choose not to eat certain foods.

Not eating one or two foods won't do any harm. No single food is essential to a healthy diet because its nutrients can be obtained from many other foods. However, the more foods that are excluded, the more difficult it is to ensure that adequate amounts of all nutrients are eaten.

VEGETARIANS choose not to eat meat and poultry but most eat milk, yogurt, cheese and eggs as well as fruits, vegetables, cereals and nuts. Some eat fish, others don't.

All vegetarians can easily get enough of all the nutrients they need without eating meat. They usually know a great deal about nutrition and take care to eat healthily. It used to be thought that they might be short of iron because this nutrient is more easily absorbed from meats than vegetable and cereal foods. However, the whole area of iron and anaemia is complicated. Very often, when people who are thought to be iron deficient are given supplements, they do not make any more haemoglobin (the oxygen-carrying part of blood). And there is some evidence, not confirmed, that people with so-called iron deficiency are less likely to have heart disease than others. Of course, very low levels of iron in the body are accompanied by the symptoms of anaemia and need to be corrected, but few people nowadays suffer from this problem.

VEGANS won't eat any foods of animal origin. Not only do they exclude meats and fish, but also milk, yogurt, cheese, eggs, cream and butter, and ingredients like gelatine and cochineal. They do eat fruits, vegetables, nuts and cereals. As long as they eat enough to satisfy energy needs — which is not always easy because the diet is bulky — vegans are healthy and obtain nearly all nutrients.

The one nutrient which may cause problems is vitamin B_{12} because it is only ever found in animal foods, although some can be made by the bacteria in the human gut and absorbed. Vegans are usually recommended to have B_{12} tablets or injections 2 or 3 times a year. Vegans have no problem about getting enough dietary fibre, and they very rarely suffer from overweight.

Vegan children need to be monitored carefully because they may find it more difficult than adults to eat enough energy. The foods vegans will eat are rich in fibre and contain a lot of water, so a large bulk has to be eaten to get enough nutrients. Those of us who are overweight could learn the value of water and fibre from the example of vegans!

EVEN MORE RESTRICTED DIETS are definitely not satisfactory. Quite apart from the fact that they are boring, they're not nutritionally adequate. For 'religious' reasons, some people decide to eat nothing but rice or fruits. Sooner or later they become ill.

ATHLETES and those with high energy needs simply need more energy than the rest of us. They don't need more protein or minerals (except sodium to replace losses in sweat), but simply by eating more of their normal food they will be getting more of these nutrients.

Weight-lifters and others involved in 'explosive' events, who need to develop large muscles, need more protein than others, but the kind of normal diet we eat in this country will contain more than enough. There is no physiological case for eating beef steak for breakfast, lunch and dinner. Whether there is

a psychological benefit is another matter altogether.

PREGNANCY is probably the one time in a woman's life when she becomes very conscious of what she eats because she is responsible not only for her own health but also for that of her baby.

It is commonsense that the baby needs nutrients and energy to make his organs and tissues, and to enable the chemical reactions of life to go on, but the amount of energy is often over-estimated. The old adage of eating for two is true if you remember it's one adult and a tiny baby. Anyone who takes the liberty of eating for two adults will not only find the extra weight difficult to remove after the birth, but will also run a greater risk of developing complications during pregnancy.

It is equally bad to restrict food intake to try to control the mother's weight. There may be rare exceptions, but in these cases food restriction must be initiated and controlled by a doctor. The danger of not eating enough during pregnancy is not only that the baby's growth and development *may* be impaired, but more likely that the mother will find it difficult to breast feed adequately.

It used to be thought that a pregnant woman didn't need to eat extra food until the second half of her pregnancy. New research casts doubt on this. First of all, it seems to be important that a woman is well nourished before she becomes pregnant. Secondly, hormone changes in the pregnant woman's body mean that she can store energy and more protein than usual during the first four months. Other hormone changes later on mean that these stores can be transferred to the foetus during the time when nutrient and energy needs are highest. The basic healthy eating plan we've outlined will provide enough protein for these extra needs, but the normal weight woman should aim to eat 200–300 kcals (800–1200 kJ) a day more than she needs to maintain body weight right from the start of pregnancy. If these come from the foods detailed on page 20 the extra vitamins needed will be provided.

The third finding is that a woman adapts to absorb a higher proportion of the calcium and iron in food than when she is not pregnant. So although need for these two nutrients does increase in pregnancy, most of the extra will be provided without the woman changing her diet. Even so, it seems sensible to take part of the extra energy as milk, cheese and yogurt.

Some doctors prescribe extra iron and folic acid as tablets during pregnancy but a good diet with liver or kidney at least twice a week and lots of green vegetables should be taken too. These foods, wholemeal bread and fruits will help prevent constipation.

Regrettably, there is still no more sophisticated cure for morning sickness than taking life slowly and eating a few plain biscuits or toast before getting up. Recent research suggests this could be because cereal-based foods contain vitamin B_6. Some people find it helps to eat several small meals a day rather than 3 main meals. Alcohol and cigarettes should be avoided during pregnancy as far as possible.

BREAST FEEDING The benefits of breast feeding a baby are dealt with opposite, but it is clear that breast milk has to be a complete food for the infant. It has to contain every nutrient and enough energy to allow rapid growth. During breast feeding, the extra nutrients and energy needed will ideally be supplied from the food the mother eats, but even if her diet at this time is not completely adequate, the 'missing' nutrients can be supplied from her own body stores.

Compared with her diet before pregnancy, the mother needs about 600 kcals (2500 kJ) a day extra during lactation. Again, the extra nutrients will automatically be supplied if this energy comes from foods like milk, bread, fish, meat, vegetables, fruits and cheese. The calcium needs of the baby are high and an extra 300 ml ($\frac{1}{2}$ pint) milk and a small piece of cheese is sensible.

Feeding babies and young children

There is no doubt that breast milk is the best food for healthy babies, from birth to about 3 or 4 months. Many could be given breast milk during the early stages of weaning— indeed in developing countries it is normal practice to breast feed for at least 6 months.

The nutrient composition of breast milk is very different from that of cow's milk. After all, cow's milk is intended for calves which grow at a much faster rate than human infants. The two kinds of milk contain the same nutrients but in very different amounts. Plain cow's milk should never be given to a young baby.

Apart from being nutritionally best for the baby, breast milk also contains substances which help him resist infection. These are present in the largest amounts in the milk secreted during the first week after birth (colostrum). When the baby is about two weeks old he begins to make his own defences against infection. So, even if breast feeding cannot be continued for more than two weeks, this will be a great help to the infant. Because breast milk is virtually sterile the baby has additional protection against infection.

This protection is important for the very young baby. Infections usually cause diarrhoea and the loss of body water is more serious the younger the baby.

Breast milk is always at the right temperature—body temperature—and the close contact between mother and infant during feeding is important for the future relationship between the two.

As if that were not enough incentive to try breast feeding, lactation can do a great deal to help the mother regain her pre-pregnancy weight. Breast milk production is an energy-intensive process and the fat stores deposited during pregnancy are used to form parts of the milk. Finally, breast feeding is also very convenient. No matter where you are when the baby feels hungry, he can be fed within a matter of minutes.

BOTTLE FEEDING The vast majority of women can breast feed if they choose to, and if they persevere for a few days. For others it is either physiologically impossible or medically inadvisable, and some simply don't want to breast feed.

For these mothers' babies there are many milk formulae on the market. Almost all are based on cow's milk which has been changed to a greater or lesser extent to make it more like human milk.

The most highly adapted formulae, in which the protein, fat and minerals have been changed, are most suitable for the youngest babies. As the infant develops, his kidneys and liver and other control mechanisms become more mature and can cope with a formula which is less adapted to his exact needs. Such formulae are intended for infants from about 4 months of age. The best person to advise on the most suitable formula for individual infants is the paediatrician or health visitor.

WEANING on to solids is generally better not started before 4 months of age, and even then it is a gradual process taking many weeks before the infant is eating the full range of foods. The initial introduction of a teaspoon or two of solids is intended more to accustom the infant to different colours, tastes and textures than to nourish him. Milk still fulfils the latter function.

The very first foods are thick liquids like egg yolk and cereal-thickened milk. It is better to use puréed rice and maize or products based on these until the baby is about 6 months old because this may help to prevent some children developing coeliac disease. This is an inability to digest and absorb a protein in wheat.

The weaning period is a very important time in the eating experience of the child. If it is happy for both mother and infant, the child is unlikely to become a temperamental eater later on, and if many different foods are tried in the first year the child will probably grow up willing to try new foods. If the child's diet is varied, it is more likely to be well-balanced and nutritionally sound, and a varied diet is more interesting.

Children often go through a phase of not eating certain foods, and even of not eating at all. If one food is rejected, don't force it, but try again a week later. Even the most adventurous of us have one or two food dislikes! Coping with total food refusal is more difficult because most mothers are convinced their children will become desperately ill if they don't eat for a day. They won't. The most important thing for the mother to do is to keep calm and refuse to be 'bribed'. Give the child his normal meal, wait a reasonable time and if he hasn't eaten it, take the plate away. He may well get hungry an hour later but the worst thing you can do is give in and offer sweets, chocolate or biscuits. That is the thin end of the wedge.

Very few children deliberately starve themselves at the age of two or five. But if a child still isn't eating after three days, medical help should be sought.

RULES AND HABITS The sooner a child learns to eat three or four meals a day and as little as possible between them the better.

Of course some 'treats' are essential, but chocolates, crisps and biscuits should not be recognised as everyday items of food. It is possible to make a rule that sweet treats are eaten on Sunday afternoon (or equivalent time) and not throughout the week. It's difficult to keep when children start school, but it's worth a try. And try to persuade grandma that there are plenty of other things besides chocolate she can buy your children. You can even try offering dried fruit as an alternative to sweets.

The first five years of a child's life are important for so many aspects of his development, not least in determining his future eating habits and attitudes towards food. So effort exerted then is well repaid later.

Cooking for health

There's a lot of truth in the phrase 'it's not what you cook, it's the way that you cook it'. Some of the nutrients in foods can be affected dramatically by the way they're cooked.

HOW ARE FOODS AFFECTED BY COOKING METHODS?

To get the cooking phenomenon into perspective, it's important to realise that the majority of nutrients aren't affected at all. These include proteins, carbohydrates, minerals and the fat soluble vitamins A, D, E and K. Perhaps surprisingly, dietary fibre is not reduced by cooking, which emphasises the point that foods don't have to be obviously 'fibrous' to be good sources of fibre. The nutrients which *are* affected by cooking include vitamin C, folic acid, a few of the B group of vitamins and fat.

Cooking also affects foods in other ways which indirectly alter the nutritional value, or 'health giving' properties. By and large, we cook food to make it more pleasant to eat. Not many people in this country eat raw meat or fish and most of the vegetables we eat are cooked too. Wheat and other cereals are cooked into bread, pasta, scones, etc.

Of all the nutrients, vitamin C is the best known for its tendency to dissolve out of foods into cooking water. Certainly a high proportion is lost in this way and some is actually destroyed by heat and oxygen. It is possible, by over-cooking and keeping vegetables hot, to remove all the vitamin C they started out with. This is by no means inevitable, however, but more of that later.

Cooking does have some positive nutritional aspects too. If you've ever compared the amount (weight) of raw and cooked cabbage you can happily eat—assuming you like cabbage in the first place—you know you can probably eat twice as much of the cooked version as the raw. If half the vitamin C present in the raw food is lost by cooking,

you'll finish up with the same amount of the vitamin in both raw and cooked cabbage.

Cooking has another advantage in that it makes inedible foods edible. Some of the foods we eat contain poisons in their natural state. The best known of these is probably red kidney beans, but boiling for ten minutes destroys the poison and makes the beans perfectly wholesome. Cooking also destroys many food-poisoning bacteria. Whether we like it or not they do exist and most people have suffered the ill effects of a bout of food poisoning at one time or another. The most common type is caused by salmonella organisms. Fortunately these 'bugs' are easily destroyed by heat and, once dead, can do no harm.

Salmonellae occur mainly on the surfaces of carcass meats and in poultry. As long as poultry is cooked so that none of the flesh is raw and pink in colour, the salmonellae will be killed. It is important to thaw frozen poultry thoroughly before cooking to be sure it is completely cooked. In the case of whole joints of meat, because any bacteria are on the surface, they are bound to be heated sufficiently to be killed. It doesn't matter if the inner flesh is still underdone—there aren't any bacteria there.

Other kinds of food-poisoning organisms, such as staphylococcus, produce toxin only when they are alive, but the poison remains a danger even after the bacterial cells are dead. Foods need to be cooked for quite a long time to destroy the toxin so it is important to prevent contamination of the food in the first place.

LOSS OF NUTRIENTS

Normal cooking has no effect on most nutrients but does affect a few vitamins and fat. The relevant vitamins are found in vegetables, as well as other foods, so some loss caused by leaching into the cooking water and heat destruction is inevitable. Losses can be kept to a minimum by using as little water as possible and by cooking for the shortest time necessary. The volume of water used is more important than the cooking time, and bicarbonate of soda is not necessary for the green colour to be retained. It destroys vitamin C very quickly.

Vegetables, and other foods, should be eaten as soon as possible after they are cooked. Keeping them hot for more than half an hour means that more vitamin C is destroyed. The finer vegetables are chopped, the greater are the losses, so leaf spinach retains vitamin C better than chopped. Many people are taught to keep vegetable cooking water to use in gravy or sauces. There's no harm in doing so, but it isn't going to add much to the total daily nutrient intake. When you consider that a small glass of orange juice provides 30 mg vitamin C, the odd milligram contained in vegetable water is really not that significant.

FRYING OR GRILLING?

The most dramatic effect of cooking foods is seen in the fat content. Many people know that white fish has almost no fat and is a relatively low energy food. What they completely forget about is the effect of adding batter or crumbs *and then frying it*. Some foods absorb all the fat they are given, and the energy content shoots up. Examples are mashed potato, onions, mushrooms, foods coated with breadcrumbs and batter, and bread.

A fish cake (which contains potato) might contain 60 kcals (250 kJ) and almost no fat before cooking. If it is brushed with a teaspoon of oil and grilled it will contain 5 g fat and 100 kcals (400 kJ). However, if it's *fried* in fat or oil it will absorb 11 g fat and have an energy content of 160 kcals (670 kJ)—quite a difference from the original potato and fish cake!

Such examples have given rise to the advice to grill rather than fry. This is only sensible if you don't smother the food with fat before

grilling! Although fat loss may be slightly greater after grilling, some raw foods, with a moderate or high fat content to start with, such as mince, sausages and bacon, will lose fat whether they are grilled or fried.

CUTTING DOWN THE FAT

How many times have you seen someone who is trying to slim in a restaurant, choose a salad only to cover it with mayonnaise or vinaigrette dressing, both of which are high in fat (and energy)? What started out as 5 kcals (20 kJ) worth of lettuce finishes up as 100 kcals (400 kJ). A baked potato might have 200 kcals (800 kJ) and no fat. Add only 15 g ($\frac{1}{2}$ oz) butter or margarine and it goes up to 300 kcals (1250 kJ) and 12 g fat.

When you're trying to lose weight, remember that *everything* you eat and drink counts towards the nutrient and energy total and you won't go far wrong. If you forget about the extras and between-meal bits and pieces, what started out as a healthy diet is going to finish up far less healthy.

The following tips will help you to cut fat intake:

Make gravy with very little fat.
Make white sauces with skimmed milk and very little fat using the 'all in one' method.
Get a good cheese flavour without excess fat and calories by using a strong cheese like Parmesan. Buying it in a block and grating your own is better.
Use whipping cream instead of double; single instead of whipping for pouring.
Cook fatty foods like sausages and bacon very well.
Spread butter thinly—let it soften before you try!
Poach mushrooms and onions in stock instead of frying them.
Make fruit crumbles with less fat and sugar than most recipes recommend.
Always remove all visible fat from meat.
Always remove poultry skin.

Energy, fat and dietary fibre contents of foods

	Amount	Weight of edible food g	Energy Cals	kJ	Fat g	Dietary fibre g
All Bran	4 tbsp	50	140	580	3	13
Almonds	18	25	140	580	13	4
Apple, cooking	1 medium	125	45	200	0	3
Apple, eating	1 medium	100	45	200	0	2
Apple, stewed, no sugar	4 tbsp	75	25	100	0	1.5
Apple juice	sm glass	150	50	145	0	0
Apricots, fresh	1	50	15	60	0	1
Apricots, dried	10 halves	25	45	195	0	6
Avocado	½ medium	125	280	1170	27	2.5
Bacon, streaky, grilled, lean and fat	1 rasher	12	50	210	4	0
Bacon, back, grilled, lean and fat	1 rasher	20	80	335	7	0
Banana	1 medium	100	80	340	0	3.5
Beans, baked	sm can	150	100	420	1	11
Beans, broad, boiled	1 tbsp	25	15	50	0	1
Beans, butter, boiled	1 tbsp	25	25	100	0	1.5
Beans, red kidney, boiled	1 tbsp	25	25	100	0	1.5
Beans, runner, boiled	1 tbsp	25	5	25	0	1
Beef, lean, stewed	1 portion	100	125	520	3	0
Beef, lean, roast	2 thin slices	50	90	370	4	0
Beef, mince, stewed, fat removed	1 portion	80	180	760	12	0
Beefburgers, grilled	1	50	130	550	10	0
Beer, pale ale	½ pint	284	80	330	0	0
Beer, lager	½ pint	284	80	330	0	0
Beer, stout	½ pint	284	110	460	0	0
Beetroot, boiled	1 baby beet	25	10	50	0	0.5
Biscuits, cream sandwich	3	30	150	650	8	0.5
Biscuits, digestive	1	15	70	300	3	1
Biscuits, shortbread	1	25	125	530	6	0.5
Biscuits, water	4 small	25	110	460	3	1
Blackberries, raw	1 tbsp	25	10	40	0	1.5
Bran	1 tbsp	5	10	40	0	2

SLIM & FIT FAMILY COOK BOOK

	Amount	Weight of edible food g	Energy Cals	kJ	Fat g	Dietary fibre g
Bread, white	1 large slice from medium cut loaf	40	95	400	0	1
Bread, white	1 large slice from thin cut loaf	35	80	350	0	1
Bread, white	1 sm slice	25	60	250	0	0.5
Bread, wholemeal	1 large slice from medium cut loaf	40	85	370	1	3.5
Bread, wholemeal	1 large slice from thin cut loaf	35	75	320	0	3
Bread, wholemeal	1 sm slice	25	55	230	0	2
Broccoli	3 spears	100	20	100	0	3.5
Butter	1 tsp	5	40	150	4	0
Cabbage, raw	1 portion	50	10	45	0	1.5
Cabbage, boiled	1 portion	75	15	60	0	2
Carrots, raw	1 medium	50	10	50	0	1.5
Carrots, boiled	1 portion	75	15	60	0	2
Cake, fruit	sm wedge	75	250	1050	8	2.5
Cake, gingerbread	sm slice	35	130	550	4	0.5
Cake, sponge without fat	medium slice	35	105	450	2	0.5
Cake, sponge with fat	medium slice	35	160	680	9	0.5
Cake, sponge, with cream and jam	medium slice	40	130	540	7	0.5
Cauliflower, raw		50	10	40	0	1.5
Cauliflower, boiled	1 portion	75	10	40	0	1.5
Celery, raw	2 sticks	20	2	10	0	0.5
Cheese, Cheddar	2.5-cm (1-inch) cube	30	120	500	10	0
Cheese, cottage	sm tub	115	110	460	5	0
Cheese, low-fat soft	1 level tbsp	15	65	270	7	0
Cheese, Edam	2.5-cm (1-inch) cube	30	90	380	7	0
Cheese, parmesan	1 heaped tbsp	15	60	250	4	0
Cherries, eating	10	25	10	50	0	0.5
Chicken, roast	2 thin slices	50	75	300	3	0
Chocolate	small bar	50	270	1100	15	0
Chocolates, fancy	3	35	160	680	7	0

FAMILY NUTRITION

	Amount	Weight of edible food g	Energy		Fat g	Dietary fibre g
			Cals	kJ		
Christmas pudding	3 tbsp	100	300	1280	12	2
Cider, dry	½ pint	284	95	430	0	0
Coconut, fresh	2.5-cm (1-inch) cube	30	105	430	11	4
Coconut, desiccated	1 tbsp	15	90	370	9	3.5
Cod, baked	1 steak	100	95	400	0	0
Cod, fried in batter	1 portion	100	200	830	10	0
Cod, poached	1 portion	100	95	400	0	0
Corned beef	2 thin slices	50	105	450	6	0
Corn flakes	4 tbsp	25	95	390	0	2.5
Cranberries	1 tbsp	25	55	15	0	1
Cranberry sauce	1 tbsp	25	65	270	0	1
Cream, double	1 tbsp	15	65	270	7	0
Cream, whipping	1 tbsp	15	50	215	5	0
Cream, single	1 tbsp	15	30	130	3	0
Cream, soured	1 tbsp	15	30	130	3	0
Cucumber	5-cm (2-inch) length	50	5	20	0	0
Currants, fresh	1 tbsp	25	5	20	0	2
Currants, dried	1 tbsp	25	60	260	0	2
Custard powder	1 tsp	5	20	75	0	0
Custard, made with powder, milk and sugar	1 portion	75	90	380	3	0
Custard, made with skimmed milk and artificial sweetener	1 portion	75	40	170	0	0
Damsons	1	25	10	40	0	1
Dates, dried	5	25	65	260	0	2
Doughnuts, jam	1	50	175	730	8	0
Doughnuts, cream	1	50	170	710	8	0
Dripping	1 tbsp	12	100	440	12	0
Duck, roast, flesh only	½ small	100	190	790	10	0
Duck, roast, meat, skin and fat	½ small	180	610	2530	52	0
Dumpling	1	100	210	890	12	0
Egg, boiled	1 size 3	60	90	370	6	0

	Amount	Weight of edible food g	Energy Cals	kJ	Fat g	Dietary fibre g
Egg, fried	1 size 3	60	140	580	12	0
Egg, poached	1 size 3	60	90	370	6	0
Egg, omelette	2 eggs	150	285	1180	25	0
Egg, scrambled	2 eggs	150	370	1530	34	0
Egg white	1	40	15	60	0	0
Egg yolk	1	20	70	280	6	0
Fish cakes, grilled	1	50	55	240	0	0
Fish cakes, fried	1	50	95	390	5	0
Fish fingers, grilled	1	30	55	225	2	0
Fish fingers, fried	1	30	70	290	4	0
Flour, plain, white	1 level tbsp	15	50	220	0	0.5
Flour, strong plain white	1 level tbsp	15	50	220	0	0.5
Flour, wholemeal	1 level tbsp	15	50	220	0	1.5
French dressing	1 tbsp	15	100	420	11	0
Gammon, boiled, lean	3 thin slices	100	165	700	5	0
Gammon, boiled, lean and fat	3 thin slices	100	270	1120	19	0
Gelatine	1 level tsp	5	15	60	0	0
Gin	single	25	55	230	0	0
Gooseberries	1 tbsp	25	5	20	0	1
Grapefruit	½ medium	75	15	60	0	0.5
Grapefruit juice	sm glass	150	45	200	0	0
Grapes	15	35	20	90	0	0.5
Haddock, fried in batter	1 portion	100	200	830	10	0
Haddock, poached	1 portion	100	85	400	0	0
Halibut, steamed	1 steak	125	120	550	4	0
Ham, lean	1 thin slice	30	35	150	2	0
Hazelnuts	10	10	40	160	4	0.5
Herring, grilled	1	100	235	970	18	0
Honey	1 tbsp	20	60	240	0	0
Ice cream	1 portion	75	120	520	6	0
Jam	1 tbsp	25	65	280	0	0

	Amount	Weight of edible food g	Energy Cals	kJ	Fat g	Dietary fibre g
Jelly, made up	¼ pint	140	85	350	0	0
Kidneys, stewed	1 lamb's	35	45	190	1	0
Kidneys, fried	1 lamb's	35	55	230	2	0
Kippers, 'raw' or grilled	1 fillet	50	100	420	6	0
Lamb, leg, roast, lean	2 thin slices	50	95	400	5	0
Lamb, leg, roast, lean and fat	2 thin slices	50	130	550	9	0
Lamb, chump chop, lean only	1	60	130	550	6	0
Lamb, chump chop, lean and fat	1	80	300	1250	28	0
Lamb, breast. roast, lean and fat	3 thin slices	75	330	1350	30	0
Lard	1 tsp	5	45	180	5	0
Leeks, boiled	1 large	120	30	130	0	3
Lemon	1 medium	120	20	80	0	0
Lemon juice	1 tbsp	15	1	5	0	0
Lemonade	1 glass	200	40	180	0	0
Lettuce	5 leaves	10	1	5	0	0
Liqueurs	1 glass	20	55	230	0	0
Liver, stewed	2 thin slices	40	75	320	4	0
Liver, fried	2 thin slices	40	90	390	6	0
Liver pâté	1 portion	50	160	650	11	0
Liver sausage	1 portion	50	160	650	11	0
Low-fat spread	1 tsp	5	20	80	2	0
Luncheon meat	2 thin slices	50	160	650	13	0
Macaroni, boiled	1 tbsp	25	30	125	0	0.5
Mackerel, grilled	1	125	280	1150	20	0
Mackerel, fried	1	125	280	1150	20	0
Mandarin oranges	3 tbsp	75	30	180	0	0.5
Margarine	1 tsp	5	40	150	4	0
Marmalade	1 tsp	5	25	110	0	0
Marrow	1 portion	100	10	40	0	0.5
Marzipan		25	125	530	7	2
Mayonnaise	1 tbsp	15	110	440	12	0
Melon, honeydew	1 wedge	150	30	135	0	1.5

SLIM & FIT FAMILY COOK BOOK

	Amount	Weight of edible food g	Energy		Fat g	Dietary fibre g
			Cals	kJ		
Melon, water	1 wedge	150	30	135	0	1.5
Milk, whole	½ pint	284	190	770	11	0
Milk, skimmed	½ pint	284	100	400	0	0
Milk, dried, skimmed	1 tbsp	10	35	150	0	0
Milk, condensed, sweetened, skimmed	1 tbsp	15	40	170	0	0
Milk, evaporated, whole	1 tbsp	15	25	100	1	0
Mincemeat	1 tbsp	20	45	230	1	0.5
Muesli	1 tbsp	20	75	310	2	1.5
Mushrooms, fried	10 button	75	150	650	17	2
Oatmeal, raw	1 tbsp	10	40	170	1	0.5
Oil	1 tbsp	15	135	550	15	0
Onions, boiled	1 medium	90	25	100	0	1.5
Onions, fried	½ medium	25	85	350	8	1
Orange	1	100	35	150	0	2
Orange juice	sm glass	150	60	240	0	0
Parsley		25	5	25	0	2.5
Parsnips, boiled	1 medium	110	60	260	0	4
Pastry, choux, baked	3 sm profiteroles	30	95	400	6	0.5
Pastry, flaky, baked		25	160	670	12	0.5
Pastry, shortcrust, baked	1 tart case	20	110	460	7	0.5
Peaches, fresh	1	100	35	160	0	1.5
Peanuts	1 tbsp	25	140	590	12	2
Peanut butter	1 tbsp	15	95	390	8	1
Pear, fresh	1	125	50	220	0	3
Peas, fresh or frozen, boiled	1 tbsp	25	15	60	0	2
Peas, dried, cooked	1 tbsp	25	25	100	0	2
Peppers, raw	1	50	10	40	0	1
Pheasant, roast	2 thin slices	50	110	450	5	0
Pilchards	1	25	30	130	1	0
Pineapple, fresh	2.5-cm (1-inch) slice	75	35	150	0	1
Pineapple, canned	2 slices	75	35	150	0	1
Plaice, fried in breadcrumbs	1 portion	100	230	950	14	0

	Amount	Weight of edible food g	Energy Cals	Energy kJ	Fat g	Dietary fibre g
Plaice, steamed	1 portion	120	110	480	0	0
Plums	1	50	20	80	0	1
Pork, leg, roast, lean	2 thin slices	50	95	175	2	0
Pork, leg, roast, lean and fat	2 thin slices	50	140	600	10	0
Pork chop, grilled, lean only	1	50	90	390	3	0
Pork chop, grilled, lean and fat	1	60	200	830	14	0
Pork fillet	1 portion	75	135	960	3	0
Pork, belly, roast, lean and fat	1 portion	75	300	1250	26	0
Potato, boiled	1 medium	190	150	650	0	3.5
Potato, baked	1 medium	120	150	650	0	3.5
Potato, roast	1 medium	140	225	930	7	3.5
Potato, chips	1 portion	125	310	1330	14	3.5
Potato, crisps	sm pkt	25	130	560	9	3
Prawns, boiled	25	25	30	120	0	0
Prunes, dried	5	20	30	120	0	3
Prunes, soaked	5	40	30	120	0	3
Puffed wheat	4 tbsp	25	80	350	0	4
Radish	2	10	2	10	0	0
Raisins	1 tbsp	25	70	310	0	2
Raspberries	1 tbsp	25	5	25	0	2
Rhubarb, raw	1 stick	35	2	10	0	1
Rhubarb, stewed without sugar	1 tbsp	25	1	5	0	0.5
Rice, boiled	1 tbsp	25	30	130	0	0
Rice Krispies	4 tbsp	25	95	400	0	1
Salad cream	1 tbsp	15	45	190	4	0
Salmon, poached	1 steak	115	225	950	15	0
Salmon, canned		25	45	180	2	0
Sardines, canned in oil, drained	1	25	55	220	4	0
Sardines, canned in tomato sauce, drained	1	25	45	180	3	0
Sausages, beef, fried	1 large	37	100	420	7	0
Sausages, beef, grilled	1 large	37	100	420	7	0

	Amount	Weight of edible food g	Energy		Fat g	Dietary fibre g
			Cals	kJ		
Sausages, pork, fried	1 small	20	65	260	5	0
	1 large	40	130	530	10	0
Sausages, pork, grilled	1 small	20	65	260	5	0
	1 large	40	130	530	10	0
Sausages, frankfurters	1	50	140	570	12	0
Sausage, salami	3 thin slices	35	170	710	16	0
Scampi, boiled	4 large	25	25	110	0	0
Scampi, fried in breadcrumbs	1 portion	125	400	1650	22	0
Sherry, dry	1 glass	50	60	240	0	0
Sherry, medium	1 glass	50	60	240	0	0
Sherry, sweet	1 glass	50	70	280	0	0
Shredded wheat	1	28	90	380	1	3.5
Sole, grilled	1 portion	115	100	430	0	0
Sole, fried in breadcrumbs	1 portion	100	220	900	13	0
Soup, consommé	1 portion	200	40	160	0	0
Soup, cream	1 portion	200	110	460	8	0
Soup, thin vegetable	1 portion	200	40	160	0	0
Soup, thick vegetable	1 portion	200	100	420	7	0
Spaghetti, boiled	10 × 0.5-metre (18-inch) strands	100	115	440	0	1
Spinach, boiled	1 portion	120	35	150	0	7
Spring greens, boiled	1 portion	120	15	50	0	4
Strawberries	10	100	25	110	0	2
Suet, shredded	1 tbsp	7	60	240	6	0
Sugar, white and brown	1 tsp	5	20	80	0	0
Sultanas	1 tbsp	30	70	310	0	2
Swede, boiled	1 portion	75	15	50	0	2
Sweetcorn kernels	1 tbsp	25	30	130	1	1
Sweetcorn, on cob	1 cob	250	210	890	4	6
Sweets, boiled	1	10	35	150	0	0
Syrup, golden	1 tbsp	20	60	250	0	0
Tangerines	1	50	20	70	0	1
Toffees	3	25	110	450	4	0

	Amount	Weight of edible food g	Energy Cals	kJ	Fat g	Dietary fibre g
Tomato, raw	1	50	10	30	0	0.5
Tomato juice	sm glass	150	25	100	0	0
Tomato purée	1 tbsp	20	15	60	0	0
Tongue, raw	1 thin slice	25	50	200	4	0
Tongue, stewed	1 thin slice	25	75	300	6	0
Treacle	1 tbsp	20	50	420	0	0
Trout, grilled	1	125	170	710	6	0
Tuna, drained	1 portion	50	150	600	11	0
Turkey, roast	2 thin slices	50	65	270	1	0
Turnips, cooked	1 portion	80	15	60	0	2
Veal, cooked	1 escalope	110	170	700	4	0
Vermouth, dry	1 single	50	60	250	0	0
Vermouth, sweet	1 single	50	75	310	0	0
Walnuts	10 halves	25	130	540	13	1.5
Watercress	1 portion	10	2	10	0	0.5
Weetabix	1	20	60	270	1	2.5
Whisky	1 single	25	55	230	0	0
Whiting, steamed	1 portion	125	110	490	1	0
Whiting, fried in breadcrumbs	1 portion	100	190	800	10	0
Wine, red	1 glass	150	105	430	0	0
Wine, white, dry	1 glass	150	100	410	0	0
Wine, white, sweet	1 glass	150	145	590	0	0
Wine, rosé	1 glass	150	105	410	0	0
Yogurt, natural, low-fat	sm carton	140	70	300	1	0
Yogurt, fruit	sm carton	140	135	570	1	0
Yogurt, nut	sm carton	140	150	630	4	0.5

SOUPS & STARTERS

Scotch broth

Served with a slice of wholemeal bread, this warming winter soup would make an excellent lunch.

700 g (1½ lb) neck of lamb, trimmed
2.3 litres (4 pints) water
salt and freshly ground pepper
175 g (6 oz) pearl barley, washed
1 onion, skinned and thinly sliced
2 leeks, washed and thinly sliced
2 carrots, peeled and thinly sliced
1 small turnip, peeled and thinly sliced
3 sticks of celery, thinly sliced
chopped fresh parsley

Put the lamb into a pan with the water and bring slowly to the boil. Remove the scum and add salt, pepper and the barley. Cover and simmer gently for about 1 hour.

Add the vegetables to the soup. Cook for a further hour, then take out the meat, remove it from the bones and cut into small pieces. Return the meat to the pan, with a generous quantity of chopped parsley, then reheat and serve hot.

Serves 6–8   225–300 Calories
■△△   (950–1260 kJ) per portion

Gardener's broth

Illustrated in colour on page 49

This satisfying soup, full of different vegetables, is ideal to serve before Cheese-grilled fish (see page 65).

1 rasher of lean bacon, rinded
2–3 small onions, skinned and finely sliced
2–3 small carrots, peeled and finely sliced
1 young turnip, peeled and finely sliced
900 ml (1½ pints) chicken stock
1–2 tomatoes, skinned
few leaves of spinach, washed and shredded
2–3 runner beans, sliced
pinch of fresh herbs
25 g (1 oz) short cut macaroni
salt and freshly ground pepper

Scissor-snip the bacon into a pan, add the onions and sauté for a few minutes. Add the carrots, turnip, stock, tomatoes, spinach, beans, herbs and macaroni. Cover and simmer for about 1 hour until the vegetables and macaroni are tender. Adjust the seasoning before serving.

Serves 4   95 Calories (400 kJ)
□△△   per portion

Tomato onion soup

Low in calories, this soup can be served before a more substantial main course fish or meat dish.

225 g (8 oz) onions, skinned and sliced

225 g (8 oz) ripe tomatoes, skinned and roughly chopped

600 ml (1 pint) light stock, preferably chicken

salt and freshly ground pepper

45 ml (3 level tbsp) low-fat skimmed milk powder

Place the onions and tomatoes in a pan with the stock and salt and pepper to taste. Bring to the boil, cover and simmer for about 30 minutes until tender. Press through a sieve or liquidise in a blender. Whisk in the milk powder and reheat without boiling.

Serves 4   50 Calories (210 kJ)
□△   per portion

French onion soup

If your main course is fairly light, toast four slices of French bread and float them on the soup before adding the cheese.

25 g (1 oz) butter

700 g (1½ lb) onions, skinned and sliced

1.1 litre (2 pints) beef stock

salt and freshly ground pepper

75 g (3 oz) mature Cheddar cheese, grated

Melt the butter in a pan and brown the onions. Add the stock, salt and pepper and simmer for about 30 minutes until the onions are translucent. Adjust the seasoning and sprinkle with the cheese. Place under a hot grill and cook until the cheese is golden brown and bubbling.

Serves 4   185 Calories (775 kJ)
■△   per portion (without French bread)

Bortsch

Serve this colourful traditional Russian soup with a swirl of yogurt in each bowl.

7 g (¼ oz) butter or margarine

1 large raw beetroot, grated

1 carrot, peeled and finely chopped or grated

1 onion, skinned and finely chopped or grated

350 g (12 oz) cabbage, shredded

2 tomatoes, skinned and chopped

1 litre (1¾ pints) chicken stock

salt and freshly ground pepper

2 bay leaves

pinch of mixed herbs

60 ml (4 tbsp) natural yogurt

chopped fresh parsley to garnish

Melt the fat in a pan and fry the grated beetroot lightly for 5 minutes. Add the carrot, onion, cabbage and tomatoes to the beetroot with the stock, salt and pepper and herbs. Bring to the boil, remove any scum from the surface, and simmer for about 2 hours until the vegetables are tender. Remove the bay leaves. Serve each portion with a spoonful of yogurt and a sprinkling of parsley.

Serves 4   100 Calories (420 kJ)
□△△   per portion

Iced cucumber soup

A perfect summer soup for entertaining which combines well with a fish main course, with fresh soft fruits to follow.

1 medium cucumber
300 ml ($\frac{1}{2}$ pint) natural yogurt
1 small garlic clove, skinned and crushed
30 ml (2 tbsp) wine vinegar
30 ml (2 tbsp) chopped fresh mint or snipped chives
salt and freshly ground pepper
300 ml ($\frac{1}{2}$ pint) low-fat skimmed milk

Finely grate the unpeeled cucumber into a bowl. Stir in the yogurt, garlic, vinegar and mint or chives. Season to taste and chill for about 1 hour. Just before serving, stir in the milk.

Serves 4   80 Calories (330 kJ)
□△   per portion

Lettuce and cucumber soup

An attractive hot summer soup to serve with a main course salad; try Mixed salad platter (see page 100).

$\frac{1}{2}$ cucumber
1 lettuce, washed
juice of $\frac{1}{2}$ lemon
little grated nutmeg
1.1 litres (2 pints) chicken stock
little chopped fresh tarragon
salt and freshly ground pepper

Slice half the cucumber. Place the lettuce leaves, sliced cucumber, lemon juice and nutmeg with the stock in a large pan. Bring to the boil, cover and simmer for about 15 minutes. Sieve or strain off most of the liquid and reserve, then liquidise the vegetables in a blender. Return the purée and cooking liquid to the pan, grate in the remaining cucumber and add a little chopped tarragon. Adjust the seasoning and reheat.

Serves 4   30 Calories (130 kJ)
□△   per portion

Mushroom bouillon

This light soup is ideal to serve before a more robust main course.

2 carrots, peeled and sliced
2 leeks, washed and sliced
2 parsley sprigs
1 bay leaf
1.25 ml ($\frac{1}{4}$ level tsp) dried thyme
salt and freshly ground pepper
900 ml ($1\frac{1}{2}$ pints) beef stock
225 g (8 oz) mushrooms, thinly sliced
chopped fresh parsley to garnish

Place the carrots, leeks, parsley sprigs, bay leaf, thyme, salt, pepper and stock in a pan. Bring to the boil, cover and simmer for about 30 minutes until the vegetables are soft. Strain, reserving the liquid.

Add the mushrooms to the strained liquid and return to the pan. Cover and simmer for 30 minutes. Adjust the seasoning, and sprinkle with chopped parsley to garnish.

Serves 4   30 Calories (125 kJ)
□△△   per portion

Tomato bouillon

For a different garnish, swirl 15 ml (1 tbsp) natural yogurt into each bowl of soup.

425-g (15-oz) can tomato juice
450 ml ($\frac{3}{4}$ pint) chicken stock
slice of onion
small carrot, peeled and sliced
stick of celery, sliced
2 cloves
6 peppercorns
15 ml (1 tbsp) lemon juice
salt and freshly ground pepper
lemon slices to garnish

Put the tomato juice in a pan and add the stock, vegetables and spices. Bring to the boil, cover and simmer for 15 minutes, then strain. Add the lemon juice, and adjust the seasoning. Serve hot with lemon slices to garnish.

Serves 4   *30 Calories (130 kJ)*
□△   *per portion*

Oxtail soup

The oxtail meat may be served separately, or shredded or sieved and added to the finished soup before serving.

1 oxtail
2 rashers of bacon, chopped
25 g (1 oz) butter or margarine
2 onions, skinned and sliced
2 carrots, peeled and sliced
4 sticks of celery, sliced
1 small turnip, peeled and sliced
2.3 litres (4 pints) stock or water
bouquet garni
salt and freshly ground pepper
40 g ($1\frac{1}{2}$ oz) flour
10 ml (2 tsp) Worcestershire sauce (optional)

Wipe the oxtail, and cut into joints if this has not already been done. Fry the bacon in its own fat in a pan, then remove. Add the fat and, when hot, fry the meat on all sides, then remove from the pan. Fry the vegetables in the fat, then return the oxtail and bacon to the pan, adding the stock or water, bouquet garni and salt and pepper. Cover and simmer very gently for about 4 hours until the oxtail meat is tender. Strain into a bowl and leave in a cool place or the refrigerator until the next day.

Remove all the fat from the surface. Re-heat and thicken the soup by stirring in the flour, blended with a little cold stock or water. Add a little Worcestershire sauce, if liked, and adjust the seasoning as necessary before serving.

Serves 6–8   *170–230 Calories*
■△△   *(720–960 kJ) per portion (with the oxtail meat)*

Watercress soup

Illustrated on the jacket

This soup would make a delicious starter before a fish or chicken main course.

*small bunch of watercress,
washed and trimmed*

15 g ($\frac{1}{2}$ oz) butter or margarine

1 spring onion, snipped

$\frac{1}{2}$ chicken stock cube, crumbled

300 ml ($\frac{1}{2}$ pint) hot water

60 ml (4 tbsp) natural yogurt

1 egg yolk

salt and freshly ground pepper

watercress sprigs to garnish

Roughly chop the watercress. Melt the fat in a pan and sauté the spring onion for a few minutes. Add the stock cube to the water. Add the watercress and stock to the pan. Bring to the boil, cover and simmer for 20 minutes. Liquidise in a blender and return to the pan. Beat the yogurt and egg yolk together and slowly add to the soup. Reheat but do not allow to boil. Season to taste and serve garnished with watercress.

Serves 2   *130 Calories (550 kJ)*
■△   *per portion*

Cream of celery soup

Sprinkle this soup with 25 g (1 oz) grated Cheddar cheese for a tasty, nutritious garnish.

25 g (1 oz) butter or margarine

1 onion, skinned and chopped

4 sticks of celery, chopped

600 ml (1 pint) chicken stock

2 bay leaves

15 ml (1 level tbsp) flour

300 ml ($\frac{1}{2}$ pint) low-fat skimmed milk

chopped fresh parsley to garnish

Melt the fat in a pan and sauté the onion and celery. Add the stock and bay leaves. Bring to the boil, cover and simmer until the vegetables are tender. Remove the bay leaves. Press the soup through a sieve or liquidise in a blender until smooth. Return to the pan. Mix the flour to a smooth paste with a little of the milk. Add the remaining milk to the pan. Bring to the boil, stir in the flour and gently simmer for 5 minutes. Serve piping hot, garnished with the parsley.

Serves 4   *120 Calories (500 kJ)*
■△   *per portion (without cheese)*

From top to bottom: Gardener's broth (*page 44*), Prawn and orange cocktail (*page 55*), Marinated mushrooms (*page 52*)

Spinach soup

If buttermilk is unavailable, use natural yogurt instead in this colourful soup; the flavour will not be affected.

450 g (1 lb) spinach, washed
900 ml (1½ pints) chicken stock
15 ml (1 tbsp) lemon juice
salt and freshly ground pepper
300 ml (½ pint) buttermilk
Worcestershire sauce

Strip the spinach leaves from the stems. Place the spinach, stock, lemon juice and salt and pepper in a pan. Bring to the boil, cover and simmer for 10 minutes until the spinach is tender. Press the spinach through a sieve or strain off most of the liquid and reserve, then liquidise the spinach in a blender. Reheat gently with the cooking liquid, buttermilk and a dash of Worcestershire sauce to taste. Add more seasoning if required.

Serves 4   50 Calories (210 kJ)
□△△   per portion

Red pepper soup

This is an unusual but flavoursome soup to serve on a summer's evening.

225 g (8 oz) red peppers, seeded and finely sliced
100 g (4 oz) onion, skinned and finely sliced
225 g (8 oz) ripe tomatoes, sliced
900 ml (1½ pints) chicken stock
150 ml (¼ pint) low-fat skimmed milk
salt and freshly ground pepper

Place the peppers in a large pan with the onion, tomatoes and stock. Bring to the boil, cover and simmer for about 15 minutes until the vegetables are tender. Drain, reserving the liquid. Sieve or liquidise the vegetables in a blender—if using the latter method, sieve the purée to remove the tomato seeds. Combine the cooking liquid, purée and milk in a pan. Reheat the soup and adjust the seasoning, if necessary, before serving.

Serves 4   45 Calories (190 kJ)
□△   per portion

Leek and carrot soup

Instead of using butter or margarine, for an interesting additional flavour, fry two rashers of streaky bacon. Use the bacon fat to cook the leeks and carrots and to add flavour to the soup.

25 g (1 oz) butter or margarine
450 g (1 lb) leeks, washed and thinly sliced
450 g (1 lb) carrots, peeled and thinly sliced
15 ml (1 level tbsp) tomato purée
900 ml (1½ pints) chicken stock
1.25 ml (¼ level tsp) sugar
salt and freshly ground pepper

Melt the fat in a large pan and cook the leeks and carrots, covered, over a low heat for 10 minutes, without browning. Stir in the tomato purée, stock and sugar. Adjust the seasoning. Bring to the boil, cover and simmer gently for 20 minutes.

Serves 4–6   85–130 Calories
■△△   (415–540 kJ) per portion

Turkish fish kebabs (page 61)

Kipper mousse

175-g (6-oz) packet frozen kipper fillets
15 g ($\frac{1}{2}$ oz) butter or margarine
1 small onion, skinned and chopped
225 g (8 oz) cottage cheese, sieved
150 ml ($\frac{1}{4}$ pint) water
15 ml (1 level tbsp) powdered gelatine
salt and freshly ground pepper

Cook the kippers as directed on the packet, then cool, skin, and flake the fish. Melt the fat in a pan and sauté the onion. Stir into the kippers with the cottage cheese.

Put the water in a bowl and stand the bowl over a pan of hot water. Sprinkle the gelatine on top and, when dissolved, beat well into the kipper mixture. Alternatively, transfer the kipper mixture and gelatine water to a blender and liquidise until smooth. Adjust the seasoning and pour into individual ramekin dishes. Chill before serving with wholemeal bread.

Serves 4   200 Calories (800 kJ)
■△   per portion

Chicken liver pâté

50 g (2 oz) butter
2 bay leaves
pinch of dried thyme
1 small onion, skinned and chopped
450 g (1 lb) chicken livers, trimmed
salt and freshly ground pepper
stuffed olives and celery leaves to garnish

Melt the butter in a pan and gently cook the bay leaves, thyme and onion for 2–3 minutes. Cut each chicken liver into 2–3 pieces. Add to the pan and simmer gently for 5–7 minutes until the liver has changed colour. Remove the bay leaves and mince the liver once or twice, using a fine grinder (the second mincing gives a smoother pâté). Season well and place in a loaf tin lined with greaseproof paper. Cover with a layer of greaseproof paper, then a layer of foil, place weights on top and chill well. Serve garnished with stuffed olives and celery.

Serves 6–8   135–180 Calories
■□△   (565–755 kJ) per portion

Marinated mushrooms

Illustrated in colour on page 49

1 garlic clove, skinned
100 ml (4 fl oz) wine vinegar
6 peppercorns
1 bay leaf
salt and freshly ground pepper
225 g (8 oz) button mushrooms
1 medium red pepper, seeded and finely chopped
4 sticks of celery, finely chopped

Slice the garlic roughly. Place in a non-stick pan with the vinegar, peppercorns, bay leaf and salt and pepper. Boil, uncovered, for 5 minutes. Strain the vinegar and return to the pan.

Add the mushrooms, red pepper and celery. Bring to the boil and simmer gently for about 5 minutes. Leave the vegetables in the liquid to cool, then drain off the marinade and reserve. Arrange the vegetables attractively on individual plates and spoon a little of the marinade over them.

Serves 3–4   25–30 Calories
□△△   (100–135 kJ) per portion

Smoked mackerel cocktail

350 g (12 oz) smoked mackerel
100 g (4 oz) celery, finely chopped
100 g (4 oz) cucumber, peeled and finely chopped
100 g (4 oz) red eating apple, cored and finely chopped
150 ml ($\frac{1}{4}$ pint) natural yogurt
30 ml (2 tbsp) lemon juice
paprika
1 small lettuce, washed and shredded
1 lemon, cut into eight wedges, to garnish

Skin and flake the fish and discard the bones. Combine the celery, cucumber, apple and mackerel in a bowl. Stir in the yogurt and lemon juice. Season to taste with paprika.

Place a little shredded lettuce in the bases of eight stemmed glasses. Spoon the mackerel mixture over. Garnish each cocktail with a lemon wedge and sprinkle with paprika.

Serves 8   80 Calories (330 kJ)
□△   *per portion*

Cod's roe pâté

Serve this pâté with fingers of toasted whole-meal bread or use to fill lengths of celery for a buffet spread.

100 g (4 oz) fresh cod roe
salt and freshly ground pepper
1 slice of bread
45 ml (3 tbsp) lemon juice
45 ml (3 tbsp) tomato juice
15 ml (1 level tbsp) low-calorie mayonnaise
1 garlic clove, skinned
watercress, to garnish

Tie the cod roe in a piece of muslin and cook in boiling salted water for about 35 minutes until tender. Drain the roe and, when cool, remove the skin.

Soak the bread in 30 ml (2 tbsp) water for about 5 minutes. Place the roe, soaked bread, lemon juice, tomato juice and mayonnaise in a blender. Add the garlic and liquidise until the mixture is smooth. This will take about 2 minutes. Taste and season well, if necessary. Garnish with watercress.

Serves 2   140 Calories (590 kJ)
□△   *per portion*

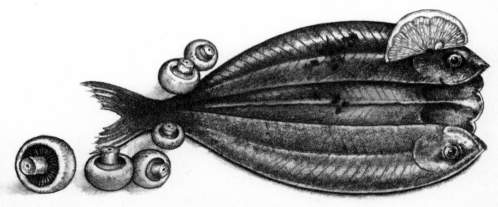

Halibut cocktail

225 g (8 oz) halibut

5 ml (1 tsp) lemon juice

½ bay leaf

salt and freshly ground pepper

few sprigs of watercress, washed and trimmed

½ small red pepper, seeded and chopped

150 ml (¼ pint) natural yogurt

30 ml (2 level tbsp) low-calorie seafood sauce

lettuce, washed and shredded

paprika to garnish

Place the halibut, lemon juice, bay leaf, salt and pepper in a small pan. Barely cover with water and gently poach for about 10 minutes until the fish begins to flake. Leave to cool in the water. Drain and flake, discarding any bones and skin.

Chop the watercress. Combine the red pepper and watercress with the yogurt and seafood sauce. Gently fold in the flaked fish. Place a little shredded lettuce in the base of two glasses. Top with the halibut cocktail mixture and garnish with paprika.

Serves 2   170 calories (715 kJ)
□△   *per portion*

Grapefruit, apple and mint cocktail

10 ml (2 level tsp) powdered gelatine

175 ml (6 fl oz) dry cider

175 g (6 oz) red eating apple

2 medium grapefruit, weighing 450 g (1 lb)

15 ml (1 tbsp) chopped fresh mint

4 lettuce leaves, washed and finely shredded

mint sprigs to garnish

Dissolve the gelatine in 15 ml (1 tbsp) water in a cup or bowl in a pan of hot water. Remove from the heat, stir in a little of the cider, then combine with the remaining cider. Core the apple, but do not peel. Dice into small pieces and add to the cider.

Remove the peel and all traces of pith from the grapefruit; do this over a bowl to collect the juices. With a sharp knife, remove the segments from the dividing membrane. Cut each in half crossways. Add to the cider mixture with the chopped mint. Stir gently. Chill until on the point of setting. Arrange the shredded lettuce in the bases of six sundae glasses. Spoon over the jellied fruit and garnish with the mint.

Serves 6   35 Calories (145 kJ)
□△   *per portion*

Frozen pineapple cocktail

An unusual fruit starter to serve before a rich mackerel or herring dish.

439-g (15½-oz) can unsweetened pineapple pieces

300 ml (½ pint) unsweetened orange juice

300 ml (½ pint) unsweetened grapefruit juice

300 ml (½ pint) low-calorie ginger ale

liquid artificial sweetener

mint sprigs to garnish (optional)

Lightly crush the pineapple pieces with a fork. Mix together the pineapple, fruit juices and ginger ale. Add 2–3 drops of artificial sweetener. Pour into an ice tray and freeze. Serve in glass dishes, garnished with mint.

Serves 4–6   55–85 Calories
□△   *(230–345 kJ) per portion*

Grapefruit and orange cocktail

When serving a fruit cocktail starter, choose a dessert not containing fruits.

---

2 large grapefruit

2 oranges

For the mint freeze

15 ml (1 tbsp) lemon juice

30 ml (2 tbsp) finely chopped fresh mint

250-ml (8-fl oz) bottle low-calorie lemonade

For the mint freeze, mix the lemon juice, mint and lemonade together. Pour into an ice tray and place in the frozen food compartment of a refrigerator or freezer. Freeze to soft ice stage.

Halve the grapefruit, using a zig-zag cut to give a decorative edge. Remove the flesh from the halves. Peel the oranges, remove the segments from the dividing membrane and chop. Mix with the grapefruit, pile into the grapefruit shells and top with mint freeze.

Serves 4   30 Calories (125 kJ)
□△   *per portion*

Prawn and orange cocktail

Illustrated in colour on page 49

---

150 ml (¼ pint) natural yogurt

10 ml (2 level tsp) creamed horseradish

Worcestershire sauce

1 orange

100 g (4 oz) peeled prawns

a few crisp lettuce leaves, washed

paprika, parsley and lemon wedges to garnish

Mix the yogurt and horseradish together with Worcestershire sauce to taste. Finely grate the rind of half the orange and stir into the yogurt.

Peel the orange with a sharp knife, removing all the pith. Remove the orange segments from the dividing membrane. Fold the prawns and orange segments into the yogurt just before serving. Serve on lettuce leaves with a little paprika, chopped parsley and lemon wedges.

Serves 3   90 Calories (370 kJ)
□△   *per portion*

Cream of lemon soup

A rich, jellied home-made chicken stock is by far the best for this soup.

25 g (1 oz) butter
2 medium onions, skinned and thinly sliced
75 g (3 oz) carrots, peeled and thinly sliced
75 g (3 oz) celery, trimmed and thinly sliced
2 lemons
1.1 litre (2 pints) chicken stock
2 bay leaves
salt and freshly ground pepper
150 ml ($\frac{1}{4}$ pint) low-fat skimmed milk
snipped chives to garnish

Melt the butter in a large saucepan, add the vegetables, cover the pan and cook gently for 10–15 minutes, or until the vegetables are beginning to soften. Meanwhile, thinly pare the rind from the lemons using a potato peeler. Blanch the rinds in boiling water for 1 minute, then drain. Squeeze the juice from the lemons to give 75–90 ml (5–6 tbsp).

Add the lemon rind and juice to the vegetables with the stock, bay leaves and seasoning. Bring slowly to the boil, cover the pan and simmer gently for about 40 minutes, until the vegetables are very soft. Cool the soup a little, remove the bay leaves, then purée in a liquidiser or food processor until smooth.

Return the soup to a clean pan, reheat gently and stir in the milk. Do not boil. Adjust the seasoning to taste and serve garnished with snipped chives.

Serves 6   65 Calories (280 kJ)
□△   *per portion*

Mackerel pâté

This starter is very quick to make and will keep in the refrigerator for a day or so.

225 g (8 oz) smoked mackerel
10 ml (2 tsp) lemon juice
1 garlic clove, skinned and crushed
225 g (8 oz) cottage cheese
50 g (2 oz) butter, softened
salt and freshly ground pepper
parsley sprigs to garnish

Skin, bone and flake the smoked mackerel. Place the fish in a bowl with the lemon juice and garlic.

Sieve the cottage cheese into the bowl and beat well until thoroughly mixed. Beat in the butter, then season with salt and pepper. Turn into four individual ramekin dishes and chill well. Garnish with parsley sprigs before serving.

Serves 4   285 Calories (1190 kJ)
■△   *per portion*

CHAPTER THREE

FISH

Grilled fish

Grilling is a suitable method for small fish, thin fillets and thicker cuts—sole, plaice, halibut, turbot, hake, brill, cod, haddock, flounder, salmon, salmon trout, trout, herring, mackerel, smoked haddock, kippers.

Wash and wipe the fish. If whole, remove the scales and fins. When the fish is too plump to allow the heat to penetrate easily (eg. herring or mackerel) make three or four diagonal cuts in the body on each side.

White fish, such as plaice, halibut, sole, cod and haddock, should be brushed lightly with oil or melted butter to prevent drying, but oily fish like herrings, mackerel and salmon do not need it.

Thin fillets or steaks can be cooked by grilling on one side only, but thicker pieces or whole fish should be turned once (use a fish slice or palette knife) to ensure thorough cooking on both sides.

Cook under a moderate heat, allowing 4–5 minutes for thin fillets, 10–15 minutes for thicker fillets, steaks and small whole fish. Adjust the cooking time as necessary, according to the size and thickness of the fish. The fish is cooked when it flakes easily with a fork. Serve with lemon wedges and parsley.

White fish: 75 Calories (320 kJ) per
□△   100-g (4-oz) portion
Oily fish: 250 Calories (1100 kJ) per
■△   100-g (4-oz) portion

Baked fish

Baking is a suitable cooking method for fillets, steaks, cuts from large fish and small whole fish—cod, haddock, hake, whiting, sole, plaice, turbot, halibut, salmon.

Wash and wipe the fish. If whole, remove the scales and fins.

Put in a stuffing, if you wish, and place the fish in an ovenproof dish. Add 45–60 ml (3–4 tbsp) milk or white or red wine and a bouquet garni (or a small piece of onion and $\frac{1}{2}$ a bay leaf). Cover with a lid or foil and bake in the oven at 180°C (350°F) mark 4, unless otherwise directed in a particular recipe, until tender—allowing 10–20 minutes for fillets, 20 minutes for steaks, 25–30 minutes for small whole fish.

Alternatively, wrap the prepared fish in lightly buttered foil and add a squeeze of lemon juice and a sprinkling of salt and pepper. Wrap loosely and place on a baking sheet. Bake in the oven at 180°C (350°F) mark 4, allowing about 20 minutes for steak and 6–10 minutes per 450 g (1 lb) plus 6–10 minutes for large pieces, according to size, unless otherwise directed in a recipe. The fish is cooked when it flakes easily with a fork.

White fish: 75 Calories (320 kJ) per
□△   100-g (4-oz) portion
Oily fish: 250 Calories (1100 kJ) per
■△   100-g (4-oz) portion

Poached fish

Poaching is a suitable cooking method for fillets, steaks or small whole fish—halibut, turbot, brill, haddock, flounder, salmon, salmon trout, smoked haddock, kippers.

Although we sometimes speak of 'boiling' fish, true boiling spoils it and fish should actually be poached—that is, gently simmered in the liquid. The cooking may be done either in a saucepan on top of the stove or in a shallow covered casserole in the oven at 180°C (350°F) mark 4.

Whole fish and large pieces are usually cooked on top of the stove, completely covered with the liquid. This may be salted water, flavoured with some of the following: parsley sprigs, a small piece of onion and/or a carrot, a few mushroom stalks, a squeeze of lemon juice, a bay leaf or some peppercorns. For the more classic dishes, you can cook whole fish such as trout and large pieces such as salmon or turbot in court bouillon (see below).

Heat the liquid until it is simmering, put in the fish, cover and simmer very gently until tender, allowing 10–15 minutes per 450 g (1 lb), according to the thickness of the cut, or about 20 minutes total for a small piece. Drain the fish, place on a hot dish and serve with a sauce made from the cooking liquid. Alternatively, serve the poached fish cold, in aspic or with low-calorie mayonnaise. Fish fillets are often cooked in the oven and they need be only half-covered with cold liquid — whether seasoned low-fat skimmed milk and water, cider or dry white wine — which can then be used as basis for a sauce to accompany the cooked fish.

White fish: 75 *Calories (320 kJ) per*
□△ *100-g (4-oz) portion*
Oily fish: 250 *Calories (1100 kJ) per*
■△ *100-g (4-oz) portion*

Court bouillon

For poaching fish (see above).

1 litre (1¾ pints) water (or dry white wine and water mixed)
1 small carrot, peeled and sliced
1 small onion, skinned and sliced
1 small stick of celery, chopped (optional)
15 ml (1 tbsp) vinegar or lemon juice
few parsley sprigs
½ bay leaf
3–4 peppercorns
5 ml (1 level tsp) salt

Place all the ingredients in a pan and simmer for about 30 minutes. Allow to cool and, if preferred, strain the liquid before using (see Poached fish opposite).

330 Calories (1380 kJ) per recipe (if made with water only, the calorie (kJ) content of this recipe is negligible)
□△

Fish bake

Mushroom bouillon (see page 46) would make a suitable starter. Balance the fish with new potatoes and a side salad. Round off the meal with Apricot and pineapple whip (see page 116).

25 g (1 oz) butter, melted
10 ml (2 tsp) soy sauce
30 ml (2 tbsp) lemon juice
2.5 ml (½ level tsp) ground ginger
four 100–225-g (4–8-oz) white fish, eg. cod, haddock, plaice
450 g (1 lb) spinach, washed

Cut four squares of foil, each large enough to wrap a portion of fish. Blend together the butter, soy sauce, lemon juice and ginger. Brush the fish portions with the seasoned butter.

Place a few spinach leaves on each piece of foil. Arrange a portion of fish on each. Add any remaining butter mixture and cover with more spinach. Wrap the fish loosely in the foil and place on a baking sheet. Cook in the oven at 180°C (350°F) mark 4 for 30–40 minutes until the fish is tender. Serve from the foil with any leftover spinach.

Serves 4 160–270 *Calories (670–1130 kJ) per portion*
□△△ *(depending on size of fish)*

Haddock crêpes

Serve Chicken liver pâté (see page 52) as a starter and finish with fresh fruits in season for a perfectly balanced meal.

For eight pancakes

100 g (4 oz) flour
pinch of salt
1 egg
300 ml (½ pint) low-fat skimmed milk
15 ml (1 tbsp) corn oil

For the filling

225 g (8 oz) smoked haddock
slice of onion, carrot, bay leaf, 6 peppercorns to flavour
25 g (1 oz) butter or margarine
175 g (6 oz) onion, skinned and finely chopped
50 g (2 oz) button mushrooms, chopped
225 g (8 oz) cottage cheese
1 egg, lightly beaten
salt and freshly ground pepper

Place the flour and salt in a bowl and make a well in the centre. Break in the egg and add half the milk. Gradually work in the flour. Add the remaining milk and beat until smooth. Heat the oil in a heavy-based, non-stick 18-cm (7-inch) frying pan and, when hot, pour off as much of the oil as possible, leaving a film. Return the pan to the heat and pour in just enough batter to cover the base. Turn over when the underside is golden —the pancakes must be very thin. Keep the pancakes warm while cooking the filling.

Gently poach the fish with the flavourings in a little water for about 10 minutes until tender. Drain, discard the skin and bones, and flake. Melt half the fat in a pan and sauté the onions until soft. Add the mushrooms and continue cooking for 3 minutes. Stir in the cottage cheese, fish and egg. Season well and heat through. Spread on to the pancakes, roll up and place in a shallow flameproof dish. Melt the remaining fat and brush over the pancakes. Place under the grill and brown quickly before serving.

Serves 4   340 Calories (1425 kJ)
■△   *per portion*

Plaice Madras

Serve this spicy fish main course with a vegetable accompaniment such as Cauliflower niçoise (see page 100).

50 g (2 oz) long-grain rice
pinch of salt
15 ml (1 tbsp) chopped fresh parsley
5 ml (1 level tsp) Madras curry powder
grated rind of ½ lemon
4 100-g (4-oz) plaice fillets, skinned
60 ml (4 tbsp) low-fat skimmed milk
freshly ground pepper
50 g (2 oz) Edam cheese, grated

Cook the rice in a pan of boiling salted water until just tender. Drain and add the parsley, curry powder and lemon rind. Place the stuffing in the centre of the fillets and roll up. Place in an ovenproof dish. Spoon the milk over and season with pepper. Cover and bake in the oven at 190°C (375°F) mark 5 for 30 minutes. Drain off the cooking liquid and mix with the cheese to give a paste. Carefully spread over the fish and brown quickly under the grill. Serve at once.

Serves 4   170 Calories (710 kJ)
□△   *per portion*

Turkish fish kebabs

Illustrated in colour on page 50

Serve this colourful main course with brown rice and a green salad.

350 g (12 oz) cod fillet, skinned
1 red pepper, seeded
2 rashers of back bacon, rinded
16 button mushrooms
8 bay leaves
300 ml ($\frac{1}{2}$ pint) natural yogurt
5 ml (1 level tsp) chilli seasoning
2.5 ml ($\frac{1}{2}$ tsp) ground ginger

Cut the cod into sixteen pieces. Place the red pepper in a pan of cold water. Bring to the boil, drain and cut into twelve pieces. Stretch the bacon using the back of a knife, cut each rasher into six and roll up tightly.

Put the fish, mushrooms, pepper, bacon and bay leaves alternately on to four skewers and place on a flat dish. Combine the yogurt and seasonings. Pour over the kebabs and leave to marinate for about 2 hours. Place the kebabs under a moderate grill, baste with the marinade, and cook for about 10 minutes, turning once until the fish is tender.

NOTE Use chilli seasoning, not chilli powder.

Serves 4   170 Calories (705 kJ)
□△   *per portion*

Haddock fillet with bacon

For a balanced menu, accompany this dish with cooked sliced carrots. Serve with Watercress soup (see page 48) to start and Pineapple salad as a dessert (see page 122).

450 g (1 lb) haddock fillet, skinned
2 rashers of lean streaky bacon, rinded and chopped
7 g ($\frac{1}{4}$ oz) margarine
15 ml (1 level tbsp) finely chopped onion
30 ml (2 tbsp) lemon juice
salt and freshly ground pepper
chopped fresh parsley to garnish

Divide the fish into four portions. Place the bacon in a frying pan and gently fry until the fat runs. Remove from the pan.

Add the margarine to the pan and gently cook the onion for a few minutes. Add the fish in a single layer. Turn it over to coat with fat, then turn the fish back so that the skin side is in contact with the pan. Sprinkle the fish with lemon juice, top with the bacon and season with salt and pepper. Cover and cook very gently for about 10 minutes until the fish is tender. Serve garnished with parsley.

Serves 4   165 Calories (680 kJ)
■△   *per portion*

Tuna rigatoni bake

Serve with crunchy Celery salad in yogurt dressing (see page 111) and a crispbread per person spread with yeast extract, for a complete, well-balanced meal.

150 g (5 oz) rigatoni pasta
salt and freshly ground pepper
198-g (7-oz) can tuna, drained
225 g (8 oz) courgettes, thinly sliced
225 g (8 oz) cottage cheese
396-g (14-oz) can tomatoes
15 ml (1 level tbsp) grated Parmesan cheese

Cook the rigatoni in fast boiling salted water until tender, but not soft. Drain. Flake the tuna into large pieces.

Line the bottom of a casserole with sliced courgettes, then add a layer of tuna, cottage cheese and pasta. Continue to layer, finishing with courgettes, and season well. Pour over the can of tomatoes. Spread the tomatoes evenly over the top of the dish and sprinkle with the Parmesan. Bake in the oven at 190°C (375°F) mark 5 for about 30 minutes.

Serves 4   330 Calories (1380 kJ)
■△   *per portion*

Fish Provençale

Served with rice or boiled potatoes, this makes a substantial main dish.

25 g (1 oz) butter
1 onion, skinned and chopped
$\frac{1}{2}$–1 green pepper, seeded and chopped
50–75 g (2–3 oz) streaky bacon, rinded and chopped
450 g (1 lb) cod or haddock fillet, skinned
15 g ($\frac{1}{2}$ oz) seasoned flour
425-g (15-oz) can tomatoes, drained
1 bay leaf
salt and freshly ground pepper

Melt the butter in a pan and fry the onion, pepper and bacon gently for 5–10 minutes until soft but not coloured. Cut the fish into 2.5-cm (1-inch) cubes. Toss the fish in the seasoned flour and fry with the vegetables for a further 2–3 minutes. Stir in the tomatoes, bay leaf and salt and pepper. Bring to the boil, stirring gently, cover and simmer for 10–15 minutes, until the fish and vegetables are tender. Remove the bay leaf and serve.

Serves 4   255 Calories (1060 kJ)
■△   *per portion*

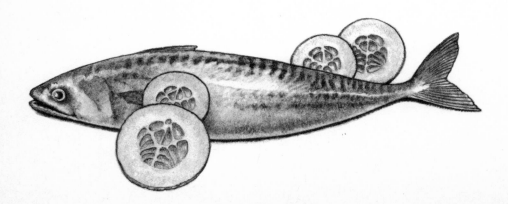

Mackerel spikes

Serve these fish kebabs with brown rice and a simple salad or Dressed French beans (see page 108).

1 mackerel, filleted
$\frac{1}{2}$ stick of celery
2 tomatoes, halved
$\frac{1}{2}$ lemon, sliced
50 g (2 oz) button mushrooms
salt and freshly ground pepper
15 g ($\frac{1}{2}$ oz) butter or margarine, melted

Cut the mackerel and celery into 2.5-cm (1-inch) pieces. Alternate the tomatoes, fish, celery, lemon slices and mushrooms on two skewers and sprinkle with seasoning. Place under the grill and cook for 10–15 minutes until the fish is tender, turning the skewers occasionally, and brushing with melted fat.

Serves 2   250 Calories (1545 kJ)
■△   per portion

Kipper en papillote

For a satisfying lunch or supper dish, serve with nutty wholemeal bread.

1 kipper, head removed
5 ml (1 tsp) lemon juice
50 g (2 oz) button mushrooms, sliced
salt and freshly ground pepper
lemon slices and parsley to garnish

Sprinkle the kipper with lemon juice and place on a piece of foil large enough to enclose it. Arrange the mushrooms down the centre of the kipper. Season and wrap in the foil. Place on a baking sheet. Bake in the oven at 200°C (400°F) mark 6 for 15 minutes. Remove from the foil and serve garnished with lemon and parsley.

Serves 1   320 Calories (1420 kJ)
■△   per portion

Rolled herrings in wine sauce

Mashed potatoes and grilled tomatoes complete this flavoursome herring dish.

700 g (1$\frac{1}{2}$ lb) filleted herrings
pinch of salt
juice of 1 lemon
40 g (1$\frac{1}{2}$ oz) butter or margarine
40 g (1$\frac{1}{2}$ oz) flour
60–75 ml (4–5 tbsp) white wine
400 ml ($\frac{3}{4}$ pint) buttermilk or low-fat skimmed milk
2 rashers lean bacon, rinded and chopped
1–2 gherkins, chopped

Sprinkle the herrings with salt and lemon juice. Melt the fat in a pan and add the flour. Cook for 2 minutes, stirring. Remove from the heat, stir in the wine and gradually add the buttermilk or milk. Bring to the boil and cook for 2 minutes, stirring continuously.

Mix the bacon and gherkins together, place some on each herring fillet and roll the fillets, securing them with wooden cocktail sticks or fine string. Place in a pan and pour the wine sauce over. Simmer for about 20 minutes until the fish is tender. Remove the cocktail sticks or string before serving.

Serves 4   600 Calories (2500 kJ)
■△   per portion

Baked mackerel

For a well-balanced menu, serve with a soup and a refreshing fruit dessert, such as Raspberry sorbet (see page 124).

4 mackerel, cleaned
2 shallots, skinned and finely sliced
4 medium tomatoes, skinned and sliced
100 g (4 oz) mushrooms, sliced
juice of 1 lemon
lemon slices and dill to garnish

Place each mackerel on a lightly greased piece of foil large enough to enclose it. Cover the fish with the shallots, tomatoes, mushrooms and lemon juice. Wrap the fish in the foil, and place on a baking sheet. Bake in the oven at 180°C (350°F) mark 4 for about 30 minutes. Garnish with lemon and dill.

Serves 4   400 Calories (1680 kJ)
■△   *per portion*

Salmon rice bakes

Salmon rice bakes make a nutritious packed lunch with a difference. Try using canned tuna instead of salmon.

98-g (3½-oz) can salmon
50 g (2 oz) cooked long-grain rice
1 egg, beaten
low-fat skimmed milk
5 ml (1 tsp) lemon juice
15 ml (1 tbsp) chopped fresh parsley
salt and freshly ground pepper

Drain the oil from the fish and finely flake the flesh into a bowl. Add the cooked rice.

Beat the egg in a measuring jug and make up to 150 ml (¼ pint) with milk. Combine with the fish and rice. Stir in the lemon juice and chopped parsley. Adjust the seasoning. Divide between two 11.5-cm (4½-inch) dishes, preferably foil. Stand the dishes in a roasting tin with water to come 2.5 cm (1 inch) up the sides of the dishes. Cook in the oven at 180°C (350°F) mark 4 for 30 minutes. Cool, refrigerate and serve cold.

Serves 2   180 Calories (755 kJ)
■△   *per portion*

Lemon kipper snack

Serve with Cucumber salad (see page 99) or a simple green salad.

225 g (8 oz) kipper fillets
2 hard-boiled eggs, chopped
15 g (½ oz) butter
15 g (½ oz) flour
150 ml (¼ pint) low-fat skimmed milk
finely grated rind and juice of ½ a lemon
salt and freshly ground pepper
4 slices of hot toast
50 g (2 oz) Edam cheese, grated

Chop the fillets and mix with the egg. Melt the butter in a pan and blend in the flour. Cook for 2 minutes, stirring. Remove from the heat and gradually add the milk. Bring to the boil and cook for 2 minutes, stirring continuously until thick and smooth. Add the lemon rind and juice and season to taste. Mix in the fish and egg.and spoon on to the toast. Sprinkle with cheese and place under a hot grill until golden and bubbling.

Serves 4   320 Calories (1340 kJ)
■△   *per portion*

Baked bream

1.4–1.8 kg (3–4 lb) freshwater
bream, cleaned

4 rashers of streaky bacon

150 ml (¼ pint) natural yogurt

freshly ground pepper

lemon slices to garnish

Without removing the head, wrap the fish in
the bacon. Put in a roasting tin and bake in
the oven at 180°C (350°F) mark 4 for about
40 minutes until tender, basting frequently.
When cooked, the bacon fat will have melted
and the fish will be a golden colour.

Place on a heated serving dish and remove
the bacon. Heat the yogurt gently, without
boiling, pour over the fish and sprinkle with
pepper. Garnish with lemon.

Serves 4–5   435–545 Calories
■△   (1825–2270 kJ) per portion

Cheese-grilled fish

Serve this tasty fish dish with Red cabbage
and beetroot salad (see page 99) for a colourful, well-balanced meal.

2 175-g (6-oz) cod or hake steaks

1 medium onion, skinned and grated

25 g (1 oz) butter

100 g (4 oz) Cheddar cheese, grated

5 ml (1 level tsp) mustard powder

salt and freshly ground pepper

Trim the fins from the fish and remove
the centre bone with a small, sharp knife.
Combine the remaining ingredients. Place
the fish under a medium grill and cook for

5 minutes, then turn and grill on the second
side for about 4 minutes until tender. Cover
with the cheese mixture and continue grilling under a high heat until the cheese is
golden and bubbling.

Serves 2   400 Calories (1670 kJ)
■△   per portion

Monk fish in a pu.rée of vegetables

Serve this unusual fish main course with
lightly cooked broccoli.

225 g (8 oz) onion, skinned and chopped

225 g (8 oz) carrots, peeled and chopped

225 g (8 oz) tomatoes, skinned
and chopped

2 sticks of celery, chopped

grated rind and juice of ½ a lemon

½ herb stock cube

150 ml (¼ pint) water

salt and freshly ground pepper

350 g (12 oz) boned monk fish, cubed

15 ml (1 level tbsp) fresh breadcrumbs

15 g (½ oz) butter or margarine

Place the onion, carrots, tomatoes and celery
in a pan. Add the lemon rind and juice, the
stock cube and the water. Bring to the boil,
cover and simmer for about 15 minutes until
tender. Liquidise until smooth, then season.

Place the cubed fish in a shallow baking
dish and season lightly. Spoon over the vegetable purée. Scatter with breadcrumbs and
dot with the fat. Bake in the oven at 180°C
(350°F) mark 4 for 30 minutes until tender.

Serves 2   225 Calories (940 kJ)
■△   per portion

Monks' mackerel

Try Oxtail soup (see page 47) to start the meal, and serve Banana and hazelnut fool (see page 115) for dessert.

---
4 medium mackerel, cleaned
---
2 onions, skinned and chopped
---
2 bay leaves
---
20 ml (4 tsp) lemon juice
---
10 ml (2 level tsp) dried herbs
---
12 black olives
---
salt and freshly ground pepper
---
lemon wedges to garnish

Place the mackerel in a lightly greased baking dish. Cover with the onion, bay leaves, lemon juice, herbs and olives. Season well. Cover and bake in the oven at 180°C (350°F) mark 4 for 30–40 minutes until the fish is tender. Remove the bay leaves before serving garnished with lemon wedges.

Serves 4   350 Calories (1465 kJ)
■△   *per portion*

Trout with almonds

Served with Chicken liver pâté (see page 52) as a starter, and Gingered apple crunch (see page 115) to follow, this makes a delicious special occasion meal.

---
4 trout, cleaned
---
corn oil
---
40 g (1½ oz) butter
---
50 g (2 oz) flaked almonds
---
juice of 1 lemon
---
pinch of salt
---
lemon twists and parsley sprigs to garnish

Without removing the heads, brush the trout lightly with oil. Place under a moderate grill for about 2 minutes on each side. Reduce the heat and cook until tender.

Melt the butter in a pan and gently fry the almonds until brown. Add the lemon juice and salt. Pour the almonds over the cooked trout. Garnish with lemon and parsley sprigs.

Serves 4   350 Calories (1465 kJ)
■△   *per portion*

Salerno fish

Mashed potatoes and a simple salad such as Cucumber salad (see page 99) make good accompaniments to this dish.

---
15 ml (1 tbsp) oil
---
1 garlic clove, skinned and crushed
---
5 ml (1 tsp) chopped fresh chives
---
6 mushrooms, sliced
---
15 ml (1 tbsp) chopped fresh parsley
---
5 ml (1 level tsp) flour

30–45 ml (2–3 tbsp) chicken stock
---
salt and freshly ground pepper
---
4 100–175-g (4–6-oz) hake fillets or cod cutlets, skinned

Heat the oil in a pan and cook the garlic, chives, mushrooms and parsley for a few minutes. Stir in the flour and cook for a further 3 minutes. Remove the pan from the heat and gradually add the stock, salt and pepper, then bring to the boil. Cover and simmer gently for about 10 minutes.

Meanwhile, place the fish under a medium grill and cook for 10–15 minutes, turning once, until tender. Transfer to a heated serving dish and cover with the sauce.

Serves 4   90–130 Calories (380–540 kJ)
□△   *per portion*

Leek and liver casserole (*page 79*)

Cod cutlet cream

Serve with brown rice or boiled potatoes for a balanced main course.

50 g (2 oz) butter
4 100-g (4-oz) cod cutlets
100 g (4 oz) onion, skinned and thinly sliced
175 g (6 oz) mushrooms, sliced
salt and freshly ground pepper
150 ml ($\frac{1}{4}$ pint) natural yogurt
dash of Tabasco sauce
pinch of dried basil
15 ml (1 tbsp) chopped fresh chives to garnish

Melt a little of the butter and use to brush the cod. Place under a medium grill and cook for 10–15 minutes, turning once, until tender. Heat the remaining butter in a pan and gently cook the onion for about 5 minutes until tender but not coloured. Add the mushrooms and cook for 2 minutes. Season to taste, pour in the yogurt and add the Tabasco and basil. Heat gently until the sauce is really hot but not boiling. Place the cutlets on a heated serving dish and pour the sauce over. Sprinkle with chopped chives to garnish.

Serves 4　　*205 Calories (860 kJ)*
■△　　　*per portion*

Cod and cottage cheese cocottes

Serve with a salad such as Dressed courgette and leek salad (see page 106) or a hot vegetable dish like Ratatouille (see page 112).

2 eggs, beaten
25 g (1 oz) fresh white breadcrumbs
30 ml (2 tbsp) hot milk
225 g (8 oz) cottage cheese
100 g (4 oz) cod, chopped
few drops of Worcestershire sauce
salt and freshly ground pepper
slices of green pepper or a few sliced stuffed olives to garnish

Add the eggs to the breadcrumbs and mix well. Stir in the milk, cheese, cod and Worcestershire sauce, season with salt and pepper and combine thoroughly. Divide the mixture equally between four greased individual ovenproof dishes. Stand the dishes in a baking tin in about 2.5 cm (1 inch) of water. Bake in the oven at 190°C (375°F) mark 5 for about 35 minutes or until set and firm. Garnish with green pepper or sliced olive. Serve hot.

Serves 4　　*140 Calories (590 kJ)*
□△　　　*per portion*

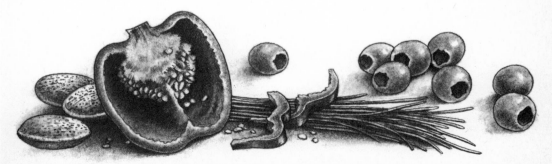

Sweet and sour pork (*page 88*)

Scotch haddock

If preferred, serve the haddock with grilled tomato halves.

450 g (1 lb) cooked smoked haddock (see pages 58–59)
25 g (1 oz) butter
cayenne pepper
lemon juice
chopped fresh parsley
4 eggs
tomato wedges to garnish

Remove all the bones from the fish and flake the flesh. Melt the butter in a pan and lightly sauté the fish. Add the cayenne pepper, lemon juice and some of the parsley. Beat the eggs and pour over the fish. Heat gently, stirring occasionally, until scrambled. Serve sprinkled with the remaining parsley and garnished with tomato wedges.

Serves 4   220 Calories (910 kJ)
■△   per portion

Soused herrings

For a balanced meal, serve this piquant herring dish with wholemeal bread and Cucumber salad (see page 99).

4 herrings, cleaned
juice of 3 lemons
90 ml (6 tbsp) dry white wine
300 ml (½ pint) water
6 peppercorns
1 bay leaf
pinch of salt
1 onion, skinned and thinly sliced

Place the herrings in an ovenproof dish. Pour in the lemon juice, wine and water to cover the fish and add the peppercorns, bay leaf, salt and onion. Cover and cook in the oven at 180°C (350°F) mark 4 for 45 minutes. When the fish is cooked, transfer to a serving dish. Strain the liquid, pour it back over the herrings and leave to cool. Serve cold

Serves 4   200 Calories (840 kJ)
■△   per portion

Tandoori fish

Serve this spicy dish with spinach, cooked only in the water clinging to the leaves.

225 g (8 oz) white fish fillet, skinned

For the marinade

1 small garlic clove, skinned and crushed
1.25 ml (¼ level tsp) ground coriander
1.25 ml (¼ level tsp) ground cumin
1.25 ml (¼ level tsp) turmeric
pinch of paprika
15 ml (1 tbsp) lemon juice
30 ml (2 tbsp) natural yogurt
7 g (¼ oz) butter or margarine
lemon wedges to garnish

Cut the fish into two portions. Combine the garlic, spices, lemon juice and yogurt. Brush the fish fillet with this marinade. Place the fish on a piece of foil and spoon over any remaining marinade. Leave for 30 minutes in a cool place. Dot the fish with a few small flakes of fat. Place under a moderate grill and cook for about 8 minutes. Serve garnished with lemon wedges.

Serves 2   135 Calories (565 kJ)
□△   per portion

Poached haddock and prawn sauce

700 g (1½ lb) haddock fillet

salt and freshly ground pepper

1 celery stick, washed and chopped

1 small onion, skinned and sliced

parsley sprig

few peppercorns

25 g (1 oz) butter or margarine

25 g (1 oz) flour

100 g (4 oz) peeled prawns

lemon slices and watercress to garnish

Cut the haddock into four portions. Place the pieces in a deep frying pan, add a pinch of salt, the celery, onion, parsley, peppercorns and 300 ml (½ pint) water. Bring slowly to the boil, cover and simmer for about 12 minutes until the fish is tender. When the fish is cooked, transfer to a serving dish and keep warm. Strain the cooking liquid and reserve.

Melt the fat in a saucepan, stir in the flour and cook for 1 minute. Remove from the heat and gradually stir in the reserved liquid. Bring to the boil, stirring all the time, and cook for 2–3 minutes until thickened. Season with salt and pepper. Add the prawns and pour over the fish. Garnish with lemon slices and watercress before serving.

Serves 4   230 Calories (960 kJ)
■△   *per portion*

Crisp-capped fish pie

Serve with Grapefruit, apple and mint cocktail (see page 54) and Spanish cream (see page 116) for a well-balanced menu.

40 g (1½ oz) margarine

100 g (4 oz) red pepper, seeded and finely sliced

100 g (4 oz) green pepper, seeded and finely sliced

50 g (2 oz) onion, skinned and finely sliced

salt and freshly ground pepper

100 g (4 oz) button mushrooms, halved

450 ml (¾ pint) tomato juice

550 g (1¼ lb) cod fillet, skinned

40 g (1½ oz) toasted fresh breadcrumbs

50 g (2 oz) Edam cheese, grated

60 ml (2 tbsp) chopped fresh parsley

parsley sprigs to garnish

Melt 25 g (1 oz) of the margarine in a frying pan and gently sauté the peppers and onion for about 5 minutes until soft but not coloured. Transfer to a 2.3-litre (4-pint) ovenproof dish. Season well. Cook the mushrooms in the remaining fat, stirring frequently, for 3–4 minutes until evenly coloured. Remove from the pan.

Pour the tomato juice over the pepper mixture. Cut the fish into large cubes. Top with the mushrooms and season again. Cook in the oven at 190°C (375°F) mark 5 for 25 minutes. Combine the breadcrumbs, cheese and chopped parsley. Scatter over the fish. Cook for a further 15 minutes. Garnish with parsley sprigs before serving.

Serves 4   310 Calories (1300 kJ)
■△   *per portion*

Baked haddock with mushrooms

Served with baked jacket potatoes and lightly cooked broccoli, this makes a well-balanced main dish.

1–1.5-kg (2–3-lb) haddock, cleaned
15 g ($\frac{1}{2}$ oz) butter
4 small onions, skinned and chopped
1 garlic clove, skinned and crushed
6 mushrooms, chopped
1 tomato, skinned and sliced
30 ml (2 level tbsp) fresh breadcrumbs
2 eggs
dry breadcrumbs for coating

Do not remove the head of the fish. Melt the butter in a pan and sauté the onions. Add the garlic and mushrooms and cook for 3–4 minutes, then add the tomato and breadcrumbs. Remove from the heat, quickly beat in one of the eggs and cool.

Stuff the haddock with the mixture and secure with skewers. Lightly beat the remaining egg and use to coat the fish, then sprinkle with the crumbs. Place in a lightly greased baking tin. Bake in the oven at 180°C (350°F) mark 4 for about 30 minutes. Remove the skewers and transfer the fish to a heated serving dish.

Serves 4   290–300 Calories
■△   (1200–1600 kJ) per portion

Baked haddock tartare

Serve baked tomatoes as a colourful accompaniment to this dish.

225 g (8 oz) haddock fillet, skinned
150 ml ($\frac{1}{4}$ pint) water
1 small bay leaf
few peppercorns
150 ml ($\frac{1}{4}$ pint) natural yogurt
1 egg
12 capers, chopped
1 small gherkin, chopped
finely grated rind of 1 lemon
15 ml (1 tbsp) chopped fresh parsley
5 ml (1 level tsp) very finely chopped or grated onion
salt and freshly ground pepper

Cut the fish into two portions. Place in a small frying pan with the water, bay leaf and peppercorns. Bring slowly to the boil, cover and poach for 5 minutes. Drain well and place in two individual shallow ovenproof dishes.

Beat together the yogurt and egg. Stir in the capers, gherkin, lemon rind, parsley and onion, and season well. Spoon the tartare sauce over the fish. Cover and cook in the oven at 180°C (350°F) mark 4 for 20–25 minutes until the fish is tender.

Serves 2   175 Calories (730 kJ)
□△   per portion

Pilchard cannelloni

4 sticks of celery, trimmed and chopped
100 g (4 oz) mushrooms, chopped
15 ml (1 tbsp) oil
425-g (15-oz) can pilchards in tomato sauce
25 g (1 oz) fresh breadcrumbs
30 ml (2 level tbsp) tomato purée
salt and freshly ground pepper
12 long cannelloni (about 100 g/4 oz)
50 g (2 oz) butter
60 ml (4 level tbsp) plain flour
900 ml (1½ pints) low-fat skimmed milk
50 g (2 oz) Cheddar cheese, grated
pinch of mustard powder

Gently sauté the celery and mushrooms in the oil for about 5 minutes until softened. Mash the pilchards with their sauce and add to the vegetables with the breadcrumbs and tomato purée. Season with salt and pepper.

Using a large piping bag fitted with a 2-cm (¾-inch) plain nozzle, pipe the pilchard mixture into the uncooked cannelloni. Place in the bottom of a 2.3-litre (4-pint) shallow ovenproof dish.

Melt the butter in a saucepan, stir in the flour and cook, stirring, for 2–3 minutes. Remove from the heat and gradually stir in the milk. Bring to the boil and continue to cook, stirring, until the sauce has thickened. Add 25 g (1 oz) of the cheese and the mustard powder and season with salt and pepper.

Pour the cheese sauce over the cannelloni and sprinkle with the remaining cheese. Bake in the oven at 200°C (400°F) mark 6 for about 1 hour until golden brown.

Serves 4   545 Calories (2265 kJ)
■△   *per portion*

Fish à la Portugaise

Accompany this colourful fish main course with brown rice. Start the meal with Watercress soup (see page 48) and finish with a mouthwatering Fresh orange custard (see page 118) for a well-balanced meal.

1 onion, skinned and sliced
2 tomatoes, skinned and sliced
1 green pepper, seeded and sliced
700 g (1½ lb) white fish, skinned
salt and freshly ground pepper
juice of 1 lemon
150 ml (¼ pint) water

Layer half the onion, tomato and green pepper in the bottom of a casserole. Cover with a layer of fish, then the rest of the vegetables. Season well and add the lemon juice and water. Cover and bake in the oven at 180°C (350°F) mark 4 for 30 minutes until tender.

Serves 4   160 Calories (660 kJ)
□△   *per portion*

Tuna and pasta in yogurt

225 g (8 oz) pasta spirals or shells

15 g ($\frac{1}{2}$ oz) butter

150 ml ($\frac{1}{4}$ pint) natural yogurt

5 ml (1 tsp) anchovy essence

198-g (7-oz) can tuna

4 hard-boiled eggs, chopped

60 ml (4 level tbsp) chopped fresh parsley

salt and freshly ground pepper

Cook the pasta in boiling salted water for about 15 minutes until tender. Drain well.

Melt the butter in a deep frying pan and toss in the pasta. Remove from the heat and stir in the yogurt and anchovy essence. Drain and flake the tuna fish with a fork and add it to the pasta with the chopped eggs and parsley. Season with salt and pepper and warm through over a very low heat, stirring occasionally. Serve immediately.

Serves 4   455 Calories (1895 kJ)
■△   *per portion*

Mackerel with cider and rosemary

4 medium mackerel, cleaned and heads removed

150 ml ($\frac{1}{4}$ pint) dry cider

30 ml (2 tbsp) chopped fresh rosemary or 10 ml (2 level tsp) dried rosemary

salt and freshly ground pepper

Wash and drain the fish. Make four or five deep diagonal slashes on either side of each fish. Place the fish side by side in a shallow dish and spoon over the cider. Sprinkle with herbs, season to taste, cover and leave to marinate in a cool place for 2–3 hours, turning once.

Arrange the fish on a grill rack and brush with a little of the marinade. Cook under a moderate heat for about 8 minutes on each side, brushing frequently with the marinade. Heat the remaining marinade in a small saucepan and spoon over the fish before serving.

Serves 4   325 Calories (1350 kJ)
■△   *per portion*

MEAT & POULTRY

Braised kidneys with tomatoes and mushrooms

For a nicely balanced meal, serve this dish with Dressed courgette and leek salad (see page 106) and boiled new potatoes or white or brown rice.

100 g (4 oz) skinless sausages
25 g (1 oz) butter or margarine
6 lamb's kidneys, skinned, halved and cored
2 onions, skinned and sliced
100 g (4 oz) button mushrooms
63-g (2¼-oz) can tomato purée
300 ml (½ pint) chicken stock or water
salt and freshly ground pepper
bouquet garni
225 g (8 oz) tomatoes, skinned and quartered
watercress sprigs to garnish

Cut each sausage into two or three pieces. Heat the fat in a flameproof casserole or deep, lidded frying pan and gently cook the kidneys and sausages until browned. Remove from the pan with a slotted spoon and keep on one side. Add the onions to the pan and cook gently for about 5 minutes until soft. Add the mushrooms and cook for a few minutes more. Stir in the tomato purée, then gradually add the stock or water, stirring all the time.

Return the kidneys and sausages to the casserole or frying pan, season and add the bouquet garni. Bring to the boil, cover and simmer for 30 minutes.

Remove the bouquet garni and thicken the gravy by boiling rapidly to reduce. Add the tomatoes and heat through. If you've used a frying pan, transfer to a heated serving dish. Garnish with watercress before serving.

Serves 4   230 Calories (960 kJ)
■△   per portion

Beef olives

Beef olives may also be served on a bed of spinach.

450-g (1-lb) piece of braising steak, trimmed
salt and freshly ground pepper
1 garlic clove, skinned and crushed (optional)
100 g (4 oz) lean ham, chopped
2 carrots, peeled and grated
2 onions, skinned and chopped
30 ml (2 level tbsp) tomato purée
beef stock
pinch of mixed herbs

Cut the steak into four thin pieces. Place each piece between two sheets of greaseproof paper and beat with a meat mallet to flatten them. Season and rub with garlic if liked. Mix the ham with a little of the carrot and onion, the tomato purée, a little stock, seasoning and herbs, and combine well. Put the rest of the carrot and onion into a flameproof casserole. Spread the ham and tomato mixture over the steak pieces, roll them up and secure each with a skewer or wooden cocktail stick. Place the meat on the bed of vegetables, add about 300 ml (½ pint) stock and some herbs. Bring to the boil, then simmer gently for 2–3 hours until the meat is tender.

Serves 4   220 Calories (920 kJ)
■△   per portion

Swiss steak

For a balanced menu, serve with baked jacket potatoes and broccoli. Slices of fresh pineapple would make a refreshing dessert to follow.

---

700 g (1½ lb) chuck or blade steak, trimmed

---

salt and freshly ground pepper

---

2 large onions, skinned and sliced

---

8 small tomatoes, skinned

226-g (8-fl oz) can tomato juice

---

chopped fresh parsley to garnish

Cut the steak into eight portions. Place in a casserole and season with salt and pepper. Add the onions, tomatoes and tomato juice. Cover and cook in the oven at 180°C (350°F) mark 4 for 1½–2 hours until the steak is tender. Garnish with parsley before serving.

Serves 4   245 Calories (1030 kJ)
■△   per portion

Chicken curry

Serve this spicy chicken dish with white or brown rice and a refreshing Cucumber salad (see page 99).

---

4 275-g (10-oz) chicken joints, skinned

---

350 g (12 oz) onion, skinned and chopped

---

25 ml (5 level tsp) mild curry powder

---

pinch of salt

396-g (14-oz) can tomatoes

---

150 ml (¼ pint) natural yogurt

Place the chicken joints in a flameproof casserole. Put the onion, curry powder, salt,

tomatoes and juice in a pan and bring to the boil, stirring. Pour over the chicken. Cover and cook in the oven at 180°C (350°F) mark 4 for about 1½ hours. Remove from the oven and boil gently, uncovered, on top of the cooker to reduce the sauce by about one third. Stir in the yogurt and reheat gently, without boiling.

Serves 4   255 Calories (1075 kJ)
■△   per portion

Frankfurter garni

Serve this casserole with boiled noodles or potatoes and a green vegetable.

---

2 210-g (7½-oz) packets frankfurters

---

175 g (6 oz) small onions or shallots

425-g (15-oz) can tomatoes

---

30 ml (2 tbsp) sherry

2.5 ml (½ level tsp) dried thyme

---

2 bay leaves

---

salt and freshly ground pepper

---

chopped fresh parsley to garnish

Cut the frankfurters into chunky slices and place in a casserole. Pour boiling water over the onions and leave to stand for 3–4 minutes. Drain and skin the onions and place them in a pan of cold water. Bring to the boil, drain well and add to the frankfurters.

Combine the tomatoes and their juice with the sherry. Pour over the casserole. Add the thyme, bay leaves and salt and pepper. Cover and cook in the oven at 180°C (350°F) mark 4 for about 1 hour, stirring once halfway through the cooking time. Before serving, remove the bay leaves and garnish with chopped parsley.

Serves 4   320 Calories (1330 kJ)
■△   per portion

Lamb hot-pot

Other ingredients may be added to this warming winter meal, such as swede, turnip or celery.

700 g (1½ lb) scrag end of lamb, trimmed
salt and freshly ground pepper
2 large carrots, peeled and sliced
2 medium onions, skinned and sliced
15 ml (1 tbsp) pearl barley
300 ml (½ pint) hot chicken stock
2 large potatoes, peeled and thinly sliced
chopped fresh parsley to garnish

Cut the meat into pieces and sprinkle with salt and pepper. Place the carrots and onions in a casserole, arrange the meat on top and sprinkle with the pearl barley. Pour the hot stock over and cover with a layer of sliced potatoes. Cover tightly and cook in the oven at 170°C (325°F) mark 3 for 2¾ hours. Increase the oven temperature to 220°C (425°F) mark 7, remove the casserole lid and continue cooking to brown the potatoes. Serve the hot-pot dusted with freshly ground pepper and chopped parsley.

Serves 4   300 Calories (1460 kJ)
■△△   *per portion*

Lemon chicken

Illustrated on the jacket

For a special occasion, serve with Dijon potatoes (see page 111).

4 chicken joints, skinned
15 g (½ oz) seasoned flour
finely pared rind and juice of 2 lemons
150–300 ml (¼–½ pint) hot chicken stock
2 bay leaves
lemon twists to garnish

Sprinkle the chicken joints with the seasoned flour and place in a pan. Mix together the lemon rind, juice and 150 ml (¼ pint) hot stock, and pour over the chicken. Add the peppercorns and bay leaves. Cover and simmer over a low heat for about 1 hour until the chicken is tender, adding a little more stock if necessary. Remove the chicken to a heated serving dish and keep hot. Reduce the sauce by boiling rapidly. Remove the bay leaves, pour the sauce over the chicken and serve garnished with lemon twists.

Serves 4   200 Calories (840 kJ)
□△   *per portion*

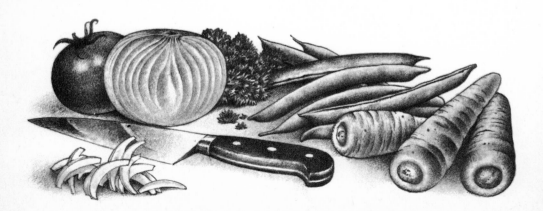

Leek and liver casserole

Illustrated in colour on page 67

15 ml (1 tbsp) oil

450 g (1 lb) lamb's liver, sliced

4 leeks, washed

600 ml (1 pint) beef stock

15 ml (1 level tbsp) tomato purée

salt and freshly ground pepper

Heat the oil in a frying pan and lightly cook the liver. Arrange in an ovenproof dish. Cut the leeks into small pieces about 0.5 cm ($\frac{1}{4}$ inch) thick and add to the liver, then add the stock, tomato purée and salt and pepper. Cover and cook in the oven at 180°C (350°F) mark 4 for about 45 minutes.

Serves 4   285 Calories (1190 kJ)
■△   per portion

Lamb paprika

Serve this delicious lamb casserole with boiled rice and green beans.

8 middle or best end neck lamb chops

175 g (6 oz) onion, skinned and minced

450 g (1 lb) tomatoes, skinned and sliced

15 ml (1 tbsp) chopped fresh parsley

10 ml (2 level tsp) paprika

pinch of salt

150 ml ($\frac{1}{4}$ pint) natural yogurt

Trim away all excess fat from the chops. Place them under a moderate grill and brown on both sides. Place the onion, tomatoes, parsley, paprika and salt in a saucepan or casserole and arrange the chops on top. Cover and simmer gently for $1\frac{1}{2}$–2 hours, or cover and cook in the oven at 170°C (325°F) mark 3 for 2 hours until the meat and vegetables are tender.

Gently heat the yogurt in a pan and add a little of the stock. Pour the mixture back into the casserole, stir in well and adjust the seasoning. Reheat without boiling and serve immediately.

Serves 4   375 Calories (1568 kJ)
■△   per portion

Ragoût of lamb

700 g ($1\frac{1}{2}$ lb) best end neck of lamb, trimmed

chicken stock

225 g (8 oz) tomatoes, skinned, seeded and roughly chopped

bouquet garni

salt and freshly ground pepper

4–5 carrots, peeled and diced

2 onions, skinned and chopped

2 turnips, peeled and diced

Place the meat in a pan, add sufficient stock to half-cover the meat, then add the tomatoes, bouquet garni and salt and pepper. Bring to the boil, then simmer gently for about $1\frac{1}{2}$ hours.

Add the vegetables and continue cooking for 30 minutes until the meat and vegetables are tender. To thicken the sauce, transfer the cooking liquid to a pan and boil rapidly to reduce. Remove the bouquet garni and arrange the meat and vegetables on a heated serving dish. Pour over the sauce and serve.

Serves 3–4   270–370 Calories
■△△   (1130–1550 kJ) per portion

Barbecued chicken

Boiled white or brown rice and a green salad make ideal accompaniments to this tangy chicken dish.

4 175-g (6-oz) chicken joints, skinned
15 ml (1 level tbsp) flour
2 onions, skinned and chopped
300 ml ($\frac{1}{2}$ pint) tomato juice
salt and freshly ground pepper
15–20 ml (3–4 tsp) Worcestershire sauce

Coat the chicken joints with the flour. Place in a pan with the onions, tomato juice, salt and pepper, and Worcestershire sauce. Cover and simmer for about 1 hour until the chicken is tender. Remove the chicken to a heated serving dish and keep hot. Rapidly boil the juices to reduce, then pour over the chicken and serve.

Serves 4   200 Calories (800 kJ)
■△   per portion

Rabbit hot-pot

Serve this hearty casserole with a green vegetable.

1 rabbit, jointed (about 1.5 kg/3$\frac{1}{2}$ lb)
25 g (1 oz) seasoned flour
450 g (1 lb) potatoes
2–3 medium onions, skinned and sliced
15 ml (1 tbsp) chopped fresh parsley
chicken stock or water

Toss the rabbit pieces in the seasoned flour. Cut the potatoes into quarters or eighths, according to size. Place a layer of onions in a large casserole, put the rabbit pieces on top and sprinkle with chopped parsley. Cover with the remaining onion and the potato. Add stock or water to almost cover the rabbit and vegetables. Cover and cook in the oven at 170°C (325°F) mark 3 for 2–2$\frac{1}{2}$ hours until tender. Remove the cover a short time before serving, to brown the potatoes.

Serves 4   350 Calories (1465 kJ)
■△△   per portion

French-style roast chicken

Tomato and onion bake (see page 107) and baked jacket potatoes would complete the meal. Cook all three in the oven together.

1.5-kg (3-lb) roasting chicken
5–6 sprigs tarragon or parsley
salt and freshly ground pepper
2 bacon rashers
150 ml ($\frac{1}{4}$ pint) chicken stock
150 ml ($\frac{1}{4}$ pint) dry white wine
watercress sprigs to garnish

Rinse out the interior of the chicken and put the sprigs of tarragon or parsley inside with salt and pepper. Place the bacon rashers over the breast of the bird, place in a roasting tin and add the stock and wine. Roast in the oven at 190°C (375°F) mark 5 for 45–50 minutes, basting every 15 minutes with the stock. Remove the bacon during the last 15 minutes to let the breast brown. Place the chicken on a heated serving dish and garnish with watercress. Season the liquor to taste; serve separately.

Serves 4   90 Calories (380 kJ)
□△   per 100-g (4-oz) portion

Braised liver

A delicious new way to serve liver, accompanied with boiled potatoes. To balance the meal, choose Leek and carrot soup (see page 51) and Baked apples (see page 126) for dessert.

450 g (1 lb) liver
25 g (1 oz) seasoned flour
4 lean bacon rashers, rinded and chopped
4 onions, skinned and sliced
396-g (14-oz) can tomatoes
15 ml (1 tbsp) Worcestershire sauce

Cut the liver into even-sized pieces and coat with seasoned flour. Heat the bacon until the fat runs, add the onions and sauté. Add the liver and fry until lightly browned. Using a slotted spoon, transfer the liver, onions and bacon to a casserole, add the tomatoes and Worcestershire sauce. Cover and cook in the oven at 180°C (350°F) mark 4 for 45 minutes until tender.

Serves 4   300 Calories (1260 kJ)
■△   *per portion*

Devilled chicken drumsticks

Serve these spicy chicken drumsticks with Spinach salad (see page 104) or wrap in foil or cling film to take on a picnic or for a packed lunch.

4 chicken drumsticks
15 ml (1 tbsp) concentrated curry sauce
grated rind of ½ an orange
10 ml (2 tsp) corn oil

The night before, remove the skin from the drumsticks and slash the flesh with a knife. Combine the curry sauce, orange rind and corn oil and brush over the drumsticks. Leave for at least 30 minutes in a cool place.

Place under a moderate grill for about 20 minutes, turning every 5 minutes. Cool, refrigerate and serve cold.

Serves 2   170 Calories (710 kJ)
■△   *per portion*

Spare ribs piquante

For a well-balanced meal, serve this mouth-watering rich pork main course with noodles. Serve a light soup to start, such as Tomato bouillon (see page 47) and fresh fruit for dessert.

1 kg (2¼ lb) pork spare rib chops (English cut), trimmed
25 g (1 oz) seasoned flour
1 onion, skinned and chopped
5 ml (1 level tsp) paprika
150 ml (¼ pint) stock
30 ml (2 level tbsp) tomato purée
100 g (4 oz) mushrooms, sliced
150 ml (¼ pint) natural yogurt
chopped chives to garnish

Coat the spare rib chops with the seasoned flour and place in a shallow casserole. Add the onion, paprika, stock and tomato purée. Cook in the oven at 180°C (350°F) mark 4 for 1¼–1½ hours.

Add the mushrooms and cook for a further 10 minutes. Stir in the yogurt and serve sprinkled with chopped chives.

Serves 4   345 Calories (1445 kJ)
■△   *per portion*

Creamed kidneys

Mashed potatoes and boiled sliced carrots complete the meal.

8 lambs' kidneys (about 675 g/1½ lb)
150 ml (¼ pint) beef stock
100 g (4 oz) mushrooms, sliced
15 ml (1 level tbsp) tomato purée
10 ml (2 tsp) mustard
150 ml (¼ pint) natural yogurt
salt and freshly ground pepper

Pour boiling water over the kidneys and leave to stand for 30 minutes. Skin, cut into quarters and remove the cores. Place the kidney pieces in a pan with the stock, mushrooms and tomato purée. Cover and simmer for 20 minutes until just tender. Stir in the mustard and yogurt. Season to taste and serve.

Serves 4   210 Calories (875 kJ)
□△   *per portion*

Barbecued steak

450-g (1-lb) piece of chuck steak, trimmed
25 g (1 oz) seasoned flour
150 ml (¼ pint) hot beef stock
15 ml (1 tbsp) tomato ketchup
15 ml (1 tbsp) vinegar
15 ml (1 tbsp) lemon juice
1 green pepper, seeded and chopped
liquid artificial sweetener

Cut the meat into six portions. Sprinkle with seasoned flour and place in a casserole. Add the hot stock, ketchup, vinegar, lemon juice and green pepper. Cover and cook in the oven at 180°C (350°F) mark 4 for 1½–2 hours until the meat is tender. Add 3–4 drops of sweetener to taste just before serving.

Serves 3   200 Calories (840 kJ)
■△   *per portion*

Tripe Provençale

Chopped cooked spinach and fingers of hot toast complete this tasty tripe main course.

450 g (1 lb) dressed tripe, washed
300 ml (½ pint) chicken stock
salt and freshly ground pepper
15 g (½ oz) butter
1 medium onion, skinned and chopped
450 g (1 lb) tomatoes, skinned and roughly chopped
1 garlic clove, skinned and crushed
pinch of dried thyme
30 ml (2 tbsp) dry white wine
15 ml (1 tbsp) chopped fresh parsley

Place the tripe in a pan and cover with cold water. Bring to the boil, then drain and rinse under cold running water. Cut into 2.5-cm (1-inch) pieces. Place in a pan and add the stock and a pinch of salt. Bring to the boil, cover and simmer for about 2½ hours until tender.

Melt the butter in a frying pan and fry the onion for about 5 minutes until transparent. Add the tomatoes, garlic, thyme, wine and parsley. Bring this mixture to the boil and boil until reduced. When the tripe is cooked, drain and stir into the tomato mixture. Cook over a low heat for a further 10 minutes.

Serves 4   130 Calories (540 kJ)
■△   *per portion*

Oriental chicken

Serve this unusual chicken dish with noodles or rice and French beans.

3 chicken joints (about 200 g/7 oz each)
juice of ½ a lemon
salt and freshly ground pepper
15 ml (1 tbsp) soy sauce
300 ml (½ pint) chicken stock
15 ml (1 level tbsp) cornflour
226-g (8-oz) can unsweetened pineapple pieces
15 g (½ oz) blanched almonds, toasted

Grill the chicken joints for about 30 minutes, turning once, until golden brown and tender. Remove the chicken skin and discard. Sprinkle the chicken joints with the lemon juice and season with salt and pepper.

Add the soy sauce to the stock and heat to boiling point. Mix the cornflour to a smooth paste with a little water, stir into the stock and add the pineapple pieces. Simmer for 5–10 minutes, pour over the chicken joints, and serve sprinkled with almonds.

Serves 3   *200 Calories (840 kJ)*
■△   *per portion*

Liver with mushrooms

For a more delicate flavour, substitute calf's liver, or for a stronger flavour and economy choose pig's liver.

450 g (1 lb) lamb's liver
25 g (1 oz) seasoned flour
30 ml (2 tbsp) oil
2 onions, skinned and sliced
2 garlic cloves, skinned and crushed
300 ml (½ pint) tomato juice
225 g (8 oz) mushrooms, sliced

Cut the liver into 1-cm (½-inch) slices and coat with the seasoned flour. Heat the oil in a frying pan and quickly brown the liver. Remove to a heated serving dish and keep warm. Sauté the onions and garlic in the frying pan for about 5 minutes, then add the tomato juice and mushrooms. Cook for 2 minutes before returning the liver to the pan. Cover and cook over a gentle heat for about 10 minutes or until the liver is tender.

Serves 4   *295 Calories (1235 kJ)*
■△   *per portion*

Lamb and vegetable casserole

If preferred, baked jacket potatoes may be served with this colourful casserole instead of aubergines.

450 g (1 lb) lean lamb, cubed
100 g (4 oz) onion, skinned and chopped
25 g (1 oz) lentils
1 chicken stock cube, crumbled
450 ml ($\frac{3}{4}$ pint) water
salt and freshly ground pepper
225 g (8 oz) tomatoes, skinned, seeded and chopped
225 g (8 oz) carrots, peeled and finely chopped
100 g (4 oz) celery, finely chopped
100 g (4 oz) mushrooms, finely sliced
4 small aubergines

Brown the lamb quickly in a non-stick casserole, add the onion, lentils, stock cube, water and salt and pepper. Cover and cook in the oven at 180°C (350°F) mark 4 for 1 hour. Add the tomatoes, carrots and celery. Cook for a further 30 minutes until the vegetables and meat are tender. Adjust the seasoning, add the mushrooms and return to the oven for a further 10 minutes.

Meanwhile, slice the aubergines, sprinkle with salt and leave for 30 minutes. Rinse, dry with absorbent kitchen paper and season. Wrap each sliced aubergine in an individual foil packet and place them in the oven to cook for the last 30 minutes of the casserole's cooking time. Unwrap and serve on a heated serving dish with the casserole.

Serves 4   255 Calories (1065 kJ)
■△△   *per portion*

Orange-braised pork chops

Serve Halibut cocktail (see page 54) as a starter and, for dessert, Walnut pear meringue (see page 122).

4 pork chump chops, trimmed (about 200 g/7 oz each)
1 garlic clove, skinned and crushed (optional)
salt and freshly ground pepper
1 onion, skinned and finely sliced
10 ml (2 level tsp) cornflour
150 ml ($\frac{1}{4}$ pint) dry white wine
150 ml ($\frac{1}{4}$ pint) unsweetened orange juice
2 large oranges, peeled
watercress sprigs to garnish

Rub the chops with garlic, if liked, and sprinkle with salt and pepper. Cook under a moderate grill until lightly browned on both sides. Transfer to a shallow casserole and scatter the onion rings over the chops. In a saucepan, mix the cornflour to a smooth paste with a little wine, then add the remaining wine and the orange juice and bring slowly to the boil. Pour over the chops. Cover tightly and cook in the oven at 180°C (350°F) mark 4 for 1–1$\frac{1}{4}$ hours until the meat is tender.

Meanwhile, remove all the pith from the oranges. Slice, discard the pips and cut each slice in half. Arrange over the onion and cook for a further 15 minutes, basting occasionally. Adjust the seasoning, and serve garnished with watercress.

Serves 4   270 Calories (1130 kJ)
■△   *per portion*

Smothered cutlets

A quick-to-prepare lamb casserole; bake small jacket potatoes in the oven at the same time for a complete meal.

4 lamb cutlets, trimmed
salt and freshly ground pepper
100 g (4 oz) bacon rashers, rinded and chopped
2 medium onions, skinned and sliced
2–3 tomatoes, skinned and chopped

Grill the cutlets for about 2 minutes on each side, then put in a casserole and season well. Fry the bacon in its own fat together with the onions. When the onions begin to brown, add the tomatoes, season well and cook for about 10 minutes. Pour this sauce over the cutlets. Cook in the oven at 180°C (350°F) mark 4 for about 30 minutes.

Serves 4   200 Calories (840 kJ)
■△   *per portion*

Curried mince

Serve with boiled white or brown rice, sliced tomato and banana, and mango chutney.

450 g (1 lb) lean minced beef
1 large onion, skinned and chopped
1 garlic clove, skinned and crushed
2 apples, cored and chopped
15 ml (1 level tbsp) curry powder
grated rind and juice of 1 lemon
15 ml (1 level tbsp) chutney
15 ml (1 tbsp) raisins
pinch of salt

Place the minced beef in a non-stick pan and cook over a low heat until brown. Drain off any excess fat, if necessary. Add the onion, garlic, apples, curry powder, lemon rind and juice, chutney, raisins and salt. Cover and simmer for about 30 minutes over a low heat, stirring occasionally. Add a little water if the mince sticks to the base of the pan.

Serves 2–3   275–410 Calories
■△   *(1150–1710 kJ) per portion*

Liver with yogurt

This is a delicious way to serve liver; accompany with boiled potatoes, noodles or rice and Lemony peas and celery (see page 104).

340 g (12 oz) lamb's liver, thinly sliced
15 g ($\frac{1}{2}$ oz) seasoned flour
25 g (1 oz) butter or margarine
175 g (6 oz) onion, skinned and thinly sliced
225 g (8 oz) tomatoes, skinned, seeded and roughly chopped
45 ml (3 tbsp) chicken stock
10 ml (2 level tsp) tomato purée
dash of Worcestershire sauce
150 ml ($\frac{1}{4}$ pint) natural yogurt
5 ml (1 tsp) gravy browning

Cut the liver into strips and toss in seasoned flour. Melt the fat in a heavy-based frying pan and lightly brown the onion. Add the liver and fry to seal on all sides. Stir in the tomatoes, stock, tomato purée, Worcestershire sauce and yogurt. Bring to the boil, stirring, and simmer for 5 minutes. Stir in the gravy browning.

Serves 4   260 Calories (1085 kJ)
■△   *per portion*

Hunter's harvest stew

This beef stew has a delicious gravy, flavoured with tomatoes and mushrooms, and goes very well with nutty flavoured brown rice.

700 g (1½ lb) chuck steak, trimmed
25 g (1 oz) seasoned flour
396-g (14-oz) can tomatoes
10 ml (2 tsp) Worcestershire sauce
200 ml (7 fl oz) beef stock or water
350 g (12 oz) carrots, peeled and sliced
12 shallots, skinned
225 g (8 oz) button mushrooms, quartered

Cut the meat into 2.5-cm (1-inch) cubes and coat in the seasoned flour. Place in a pan and add the tomatoes, Worcestershire sauce and stock or water. Bring to the boil, then cover and simmer gently for 1¼ hours. Add the carrots and shallots and simmer for a further 45 minutes. Add the mushrooms and continue to cook for 15 minutes. Adjust the seasoning before serving.

Serves 4   200 Calories (840 kJ)
■△△   *per portion*

Chicken and tongue loaf

Serve this delicious cold summer meat loaf with Dressed French beans (see page 108) and lightly buttered wholemeal bread.

15 ml (3 level tsp) powdered gelatine
450 ml (¾ pint) chicken stock
salt and freshly ground pepper
225 g (8 oz) cooked chicken, diced
225 g (8 oz) cooked tongue, diced
1 green pepper, seeded and diced
1 red pepper, seeded and diced
6 olives, stoned and sliced

Put 60 ml (4 tbsp) water in a cup and place in a pan of hot water. Sprinkle the gelatine over the water and leave to dissolve. Stir into the stock and season well.

Place the chicken, tongue, peppers and olives in a loaf tin, pour the stock over and leave to set.

Serves 4   265 Calories (1115 kJ)
■△   *per portion*

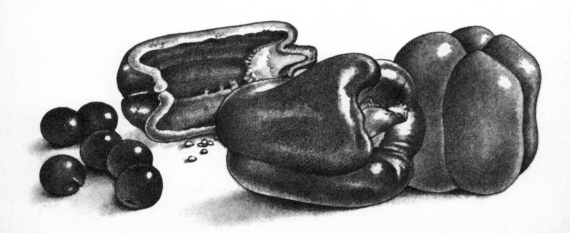

Chicken rice fiesta

A complete colourful dish for all occasions. For a well-balanced meal, serve Spinach soup (see page 51) as a starter and Date-filled oranges (see page 114) for dessert. This would make an ideal meal when entertaining friends with a summer lunch.

1.5-kg (3-lb) roasting chicken
salt and freshly ground pepper
600 ml (1 pint) chicken stock
50 g (2 oz) long-grain rice
25 g (1 oz) butter
2 onions, skinned and chopped
450 g (1 lb) tomatoes, skinned and sliced
2 red peppers, seeded and diced
finely pared rind of 1 orange
1 garlic clove, skinned and crushed
watercress sprigs to garnish

Sprinkle the chicken with salt and pepper and place on a metal trivet or rack in a roasting tin. Cook in the oven at 200°C (400°F) mark 6 for $1\frac{1}{4}$–$1\frac{1}{2}$ hours.

Bring the stock to the boil, stir in the rice and cook until all the liquid is absorbed and the rice is tender. Melt the butter in a pan and sauté the onions for about 5 minutes until transparent. Add the tomatoes, peppers, orange rind, garlic and salt and pepper. Cook for 10–15 minutes until soft.

Place the cooked rice on a heated serving dish. Carve the chicken and arrange in slices on the rice. Pour the onion, tomato and pepper sauce over the chicken and garnish with sprigs of watercress.

Serves 4   300 Calories (1240 kJ)
■△   *per portion*

Layered spinach and beef pie

For a well-balanced meal, serve a light starter and dessert, such as Cream of celery soup (see page 48) and Tangerine melon mousse (see page 122). To be certain the minced beef is lean, mince it yourself.

450 g (1 lb) lean minced beef
225 g (8 oz) onion, skinned and chopped
30 ml (2 level tbsp) tomato purée
5 ml (1 level tsp) dried mixed herbs
salt and freshly ground pepper
450 g (1 lb) frozen chopped spinach
pinch of grated nutmeg
300 ml ($\frac{1}{2}$ pint) natural yogurt
2 egg yolks, beaten
pinch of mustard powder
50 g (2 oz) Edam cheese, grated

Place the minced beef and onions in a large pan and cook over a medium heat until the fat starts to run, then increase the heat and brown. Strain off the excess fat. Stir in the tomato purée, herbs and salt and pepper to taste.

Place the spinach in a pan without water, cover and cook gently until the spinach has thawed. Drain very well. Stir in the nutmeg and season to taste. Layer the meat mixture and spinach in an ovenproof dish. Combine the yogurt, egg yolks, mustard and cheese and pour over the top of the casserole. Cook, uncovered, in the oven at 190°C (375°F) mark 5 for about 45 minutes until the topping is bubbling and golden. Serve with a fresh green salad.

Serves 4   300 Calories (1240 kJ)
■△   *per portion*

Sweet and sour pork

Illustrated in colour on page 68

Serve this mouthwatering dish on a bed of boiled rice with an accompanying salad. Use a low-calorie dressing on the salad.

700 g (1½ lb) pork fillet
450 ml (¾ pint) hot chicken stock
bouquet garni
salt and freshly ground pepper
1 green pepper, seeded and finely sliced
1 red pepper, seeded and finely sliced
226-g (8-oz) can unsweetened pineapple slices, cubed
15 ml (1 level tbsp) cornflour
15 ml (1 tbsp) soy sauce
150 ml (¼ pint) vinegar
liquid artificial sweetener

Cut the pork into 2.5-cm (1-inch) cubes and place in a casserole. Pour the hot chicken stock over and add the bouquet garni, salt and pepper. Cover and cook in the oven at 180°C (350°F) mark 4 for 1 hour until the pork is tender.

Remove the bouquet garni, drain off the stock into a pan and add the peppers and pineapple. Simmer gently for 5–7 minutes. Mix the cornflour with the soy sauce and vinegar, then add this to the stock mixture, stirring continuously until it thickens and becomes transparent. Add artificial sweetener to taste, add the pork and heat gently.

Serves 4   310 Calories (1290 kJ)
■△   *per portion*

Pork chops with creamed cabbage

Served with small baked jacket potatoes and sliced carrots, this makes a well-balanced main supper or lunch dish. Follow it up with a light and refreshing dessert such as Pineapple salad (see page 122).

900 g (2 lb) cabbage, trimmed and shredded
300 ml (½ pint) natural yogurt
salt and freshly ground pepper
4 pork chops, trimmed (about 225 g/8 oz each)
a little dried sage
30 ml (2 tbsp) dry white wine
25 g (1 oz) Cheddar cheese, grated
paprika to garnish

Blanch the cabbage quickly in boiling salted water, then drain well. Add the yogurt and some pepper and toss lightly to mix. Place half the cabbage in the bottom of a large, shallow ovenproof casserole.

Grill the chops for about 10 minutes on each side until golden. Arrange the chops in a single layer on top of the cabbage in the casserole. Add the sage and wine to the drippings in the base of the grill pan, stirring to loosen any residue, and spoon over the chops. Cover with the remainder of the cabbage.

Cover and cook in the oven at 180°C (350°F) mark 4 for 45 minutes. Just before the end of the cooking time, sprinkle with the cheese. Garnish with a dusting of paprika before serving.

Serves 4   380 Calories (1610 kJ)
■△△   *per portion*

Devilled tongue

Boiled rice and lightly cooked broccoli make excellent accompaniments to this dish. For dessert, serve tempting Banana sherbet (see page 117).

450-g (1-lb) thick slice of cooked tongue, diced
15 ml (1 level tbsp) flour
15 ml (1 tbsp) vinegar
15 ml (1 level tbsp) tomato ketchup
1.25 ml ($\frac{1}{4}$ level tsp) ground ginger
1.25 ml ($\frac{1}{4}$ level tsp) curry powder
1.25 ml ($\frac{1}{4}$ level tsp) mustard powder
1.25 ml ($\frac{1}{4}$ level tsp) mixed spice
300 ml ($\frac{1}{2}$ pint) chicken stock

Place the tongue in a casserole. Mix together the flour, vinegar, tomato ketchup, ginger, curry powder, mustard and spice to form a paste. Gradually add the stock and pour over the tongue. Cover and cook in the oven at 180°C (350°F) mark 4 for 30 minutes.

Serves 3   460 Calories (1920 kJ)
■△   *per portion*

Italian veal casserole

Serve with boiled noodles. To balance the meal, start with Grapefruit and orange cocktail (see page 55) and choose a creamy dessert such as Baked custard (see page 125) with fruit.

450 g (1 lb) pie veal, trimmed
2 garlic cloves, skinned and chopped
salt and freshly ground pepper
150 ml ($\frac{1}{4}$ pint) white wine
100 g (4 oz) tomatoes, skinned and chopped
10 ml (2 level tsp) tomato purée
2 rosemary sprigs
strip of lemon rind

Slice the meat or cut into small pieces and place in a casserole. Add the garlic, salt and pepper, wine, tomatoes, tomato purée, rosemary and lemon rind, and just enough water to cover. Cover tightly and cook in the oven at 180°C (350°F) mark 4 for about 1½ hours until the meat is tender. Remove the lemon rind before serving.

Serves 3   150 Calories (630 kJ)
■△   *per portion*

Devilled grilled turkey

Serve this spicy turkey dish with plain boiled white or brown rice.

2 turkey breasts, skinned (about 450 g/1 lb)
5 ml (1 level tsp) salt
10 ml (2 level tsp) sugar
5 ml (1 level tsp) freshly ground pepper
5 ml (1 level tsp) ground ginger
5 ml (1 level tsp) mustard powder
2.5 ml ($\frac{1}{2}$ level tsp) curry powder
25 g (1 oz) butter, melted
For the sauce
25 g (1 oz) butter, melted
30 ml (2 level tbsp) tomato purée
15 ml (1 tbsp) vinegar
15 ml (1 tbsp) cold water
10 ml (2 tsp) Worcestershire sauce
15 ml (1 tbsp) soy sauce
1.25 ml ($\frac{1}{4}$ level tsp) chilli seasoning

Slice the turkey breasts to give 4 thin escalope shapes. Mix the salt, sugar, pepper, ginger, mustard and curry powder together, rub the mixture into the turkey portions and leave for 1 hour. Brush them with the melted butter, place in a grill pan and grill slowly for about 8 minutes each side, until brown.

Mix the sauce ingredients together, then spoon over the turkey. Continue to cook, basting with the sauce, for 6 minutes. Transfer the turkey to a heated serving dish and spoon over the remaining sauce.

Serves 4   240 Calories (1010 kJ)
■△   *per portion*

Liver and ham ragoût

Serve a green vegetable such as Brussels sprouts or broccolli as a delicious and colourful accompaniment.

2 medium onions, skinned and chopped
2 medium carrots, peeled and diced
1 large parsnip, peeled and diced
2 medium turnips, peeled and diced
600 ml (1 pint) beef stock
50 g (2 oz) lean ham, chopped
2.5 ml ($\frac{1}{2}$ tsp) Worcestershire sauce
salt and freshly ground pepper
350–450 g (12 oz–1lb) lamb's liver, thinly sliced
300 ml ($\frac{1}{2}$ pint) natural yogurt
chopped fresh parsley to garnish

Place the vegetables in a 1.4-litre (2$\frac{1}{2}$-pint) flameproof casserole or saucepan and add the stock, ham, Worcestershire sauce and salt and pepper. Bring to the boil. Cover and simmer gently for about 45 minutes until the vegetables are tender.

Remove from the heat and add the liver, making sure it is covered by the liquid. Simmer for a further 10–15 minutes. Stir in most of the yogurt and heat through but do not boil. Serve from the casserole or in a heated serving dish with a swirl of yogurt and chopped parsley to garnish.

Serves 4   290–340 Calories
■△△   *(1210–1420 kJ) per portion*

EGGS & CHEESE

Scrambled eggs

Scrambled eggs should only be lightly cooked and served while still creamy.

4 eggs
150 ml ($\frac{1}{4}$ pint) low-fat skimmed milk
salt and freshly ground pepper

Beat the eggs lightly with the milk and salt and pepper. Pour the mixture into a non-stick saucepan and cook over a low heat. Lift and turn the mixture with a spatula as it sets. Remove the pan from the heat before setting is complete, to allow the heat of the pan to finish the cooking.

Serves 2–3   130–200 Calories
■△   *(540–840 kJ) per portion*

VARIATIONS
Add one of the following:

50 g (2 oz) lightly fried sliced mushrooms *105 Calories (440 kJ)*
2 skinned tomatoes, chopped and lightly fried with a rinded and diced rasher of bacon *140 Calories (590 kJ)*
50 g (2 oz) chopped ham, tongue or other cooked meat *60–105 Calories (250–440 kJ)*
50 g (2 oz) sliced cooked pork sausages *160 Calories (665 kJ)*
50 g (2 oz) Finnan haddock (or other smoked fish) cooked, boned, skinned and flaked *55 Calories (230 kJ)*
50 g (2 oz) shelled shrimps *60 Calories (250 kJ)*
50–75 g (2–3 oz) grated Cheddar cheese *200–305 Calories (845–1270 kJ)*
2.5 ml ($\frac{1}{2}$ level tsp) dried herbs or 5 ml (1 level tsp) finely chopped mixed fresh herbs

Spaghetti and egg casserole

For a complete meal, serve Chicken liver pâté (see page 52) as a starter and finish with fresh fruit.

175 g (6 oz) spaghetti
50 g (2 oz) butter or margarine
40 g (1$\frac{1}{2}$ oz) flour
600 ml (1 pint) low-fat skimmed milk
1 small onion, skinned and finely chopped
little prepared mustard
salt and freshly ground pepper
100 g (4 oz) Cheddar cheese, grated
450 g (1 lb) runner beans, sliced and cooked
4 eggs

Cook the spaghetti in boiling salted water until just tender, then drain well. Melt the fat in a pan and add the flour. Cook for 2 minutes, stirring. Remove the pan from the heat and gradually add the milk. Bring to the boil and cook for 2 minutes, stirring continuously. Add the onion, mustard, salt, pepper and half the cheese. Put half the spaghetti into a greased casserole, place some of the beans on top and then half the sauce. Repeat the layers, finishing with a sprinkling of cheese. Bake in the oven at 180°C (350°F) mark 4 for about 30 minutes until set and golden brown.

Meanwhile, boil the eggs for 5–8 minutes until hard-boiled, then shell, halve lengthways and arrange over the spaghetti with the remaining beans.

Serves 4   590 Calories (2470 kJ)
■△△   *per portion*

Welsh rarebit

Serve this popular cheese snack with grilled tomatoes.

15 g (½ oz) butter or margarine
225 g (8 oz) Cheddar cheese, grated
2.5 ml (½ level tsp) mustard powder
pinch of salt
pinch of cayenne pepper
60 ml (4 tbsp) brown ale
4 slices of wholemeal toast

Melt the fat in the top of a double saucepan, or in a bowl placed over a pan of boiling water. Stir in the cheese, mustard, salt, cayenne pepper and brown ale. When smooth, pour over the toast.

Serves 4   370 Calories (1550 kJ)
■△   per portion

Egg and potato pie

Serve with a green salad.

4 eggs, size 2
600 ml (1 pint) low-fat skimmed milk
salt and freshly ground pepper
450 g (1 lb) cooked potatoes, sliced
225 g (8 oz) firm tomatoes, skinned, seeded and sliced
175 g (6 oz) Cheshire or Cheddar cheese, grated
parsley sprigs to garnish

Beat together the eggs, milk and salt and pepper. Layer the potatoes, tomatoes, cheese and egg mixture in a buttered 1.4-litre (2½-pint) pie dish, finishing with a layer of cheese. Cook in the oven at 180°C (350°F) mark 4 for about 40 minutes, until the egg mixture has set and the cheese topping is golden brown. Garnish with parsley.

Serves 4   415 Calories (1735 kJ)
■△   per portion

Cheese and tuna quiche

Illustrated in colour on page 101

175 g (6 oz) plain flour
salt and freshly ground pepper
40 g (1½ oz) butter or margarine
40 g (1½ oz) lard
2 eggs
300 ml (½ pint) low-fat skimmed milk
1 onion, skinned and chopped
100 g (4 oz) Cheddar cheese, grated
198-g (7-oz) can tuna, drained and flaked

Place the flour and a pinch of salt in a bowl. Cut the fats into small pieces, and rub into the flour until the mixture resembles fine breadcrumbs. Add enough cold water to bind the mixture together. Roll out the pastry on a lightly floured surface and use to line a 20.5-cm (8-inch) flan ring placed on a baking sheet. Bake blind in the oven at 200°C (400°F) mark 6 for about 15 minutes.

Whisk the eggs, milk, salt and pepper together. Add the onion and cheese and mix well. Place the tuna in the pastry case and pour in the cheese and milk mixture. Bake in the oven at 180°C (350°F) mark 4 for 20–30 minutes until golden brown.

Serves 6   405 Calories (1695 kJ)
■△   per portion

Shrimp-stuffed eggs

Sandwich the egg halves in pairs and pack in a twist of cling film to serve as a delicious packed lunch with a difference.

2 hard-boiled eggs

31-g (1⅛-oz) jar salmon paste

15 g (½ oz) butter or margarine

good squeeze of lemon juice

salt and freshly ground pepper

Halve the eggs lengthways. Scoop out the yolks and sieve into a bowl. Beat with the paste, fat and lemon juice. Adjust the seasoning. Pile back into the egg white shells.

Serves 2   170 Calories (705 kJ)
■△   per portion

Eggs Florentine

A nutritious family main course, rich in vitamin A from the spinach.

900 g (2 lb) spinach, washed

salt and freshly ground pepper

40 g (1½ oz) butter

45 ml (3 level tbsp) flour

300 ml (½ pint) low-fat skimmed milk

75 g (3 oz) Cheddar cheese, grated

4 eggs

Put the spinach in a pan with a little salt. Cover and cook for 10–15 minutes until tender. Drain well, chop roughly and reheat with 15 g (½ oz) of the butter.

Melt the remaining butter in a pan and add the flour. Cook for 2–3 minutes, stirring. Remove the pan from the heat and gradually add the milk. Bring to the boil and cook for 2 minutes, stirring continuously. Add 50 g (2 oz) of the cheese and season well.

Poach the eggs. Place the spinach in a flameproof dish, arrange the eggs on top and pour the cheese sauce over. Sprinkle with the remaining cheese and place under the grill to brown.

Serves 4   340 Calories (1420 kJ)
■△△   per portion

Curried eggs

Serve this quick curry dish with white or brown rice, allowing 50 g (2 oz) cooked rice per person.

3 hard-boiled eggs

50 g (2 oz) butter or margarine

1 onion, skinned and chopped

½ an apple, cored and finely chopped

5 ml (1 level tsp) curry powder

25 g (1 oz) flour

300 ml (½ pint) chicken stock

pinch of salt

10 ml (2 tsp) lemon juice

lemon wedges to garnish

While the hard-boiled eggs are still hot, chop two of them into small pieces, and the other into wedges. Melt the fat in a pan and lightly fry the onion. Add the apple, curry powder and flour, and cook for a few minutes. Gradually add the stock, salt and lemon juice. Bring to the boil, skim and simmer for about 15 minutes. Add the chopped egg and heat through. Place in a heated serving dish. Garnish with the egg and lemon wedges.

Serves 2   430 Calories (1800 kJ)
■△   per portion

Baked eggs and mushrooms

Serve with a green salad or wholemeal bread.

30 ml (2 tbsp) corn oil
225 g (8 oz) mushrooms, thinly sliced
4 eggs
salt and freshly ground pepper
50 g (2 oz) Cheshire or Cheddar cheese, grated

Heat the oil in a pan and gently fry the mushrooms for about 3 minutes until soft. Drain and place in a shallow ovenproof dish. Break the eggs into the dish, season and sprinkle with the grated cheese. Bake in the oven at 180°C (350°F) mark 4 for about 15 minutes until the eggs have just set.

Serves 4   220 Calories (920 kJ)
■△   per portion

Cheese and onion flan

Serve this low-calorie savoury flan with a salad of tomato slices and onion rings.

4 medium slices bread
40 g (1½ oz) butter or margarine
2 medium onions, skinned and chopped
150 ml (¼ pint) low-fat skimmed milk
2 eggs
salt and freshly ground pepper
25 g (1 oz) Edam cheese, grated
chopped parsley to garnish

Spread the bread with 15 g (½ oz) of the fat and use to line a 20.5-cm (8-inch) pie dish. Bake in the oven at 200°C (400°F) mark 6 for 5–10 minutes until lightly browned.

Melt the remaining fat in a pan and fry the chopped onion. Drain and place in the cooked case. Beat the milk, eggs and salt and pepper together and pour into the case over the onion. Sprinkle over the grated cheese. Bake in the oven at 180°C (350°F) mark 4 for 25–30 minutes until the filling is firm and golden. Serve hot, garnished with parsley.

Serves 4   265 Calories (1110 kJ)
■△   per portion

Cheese soufflé omelette

Serve this perfect light lunch or supper dish with a crisp green salad or Spinach salad (see page 104).

1 egg, size 2, separated
salt and freshly ground pepper
7 g (¼ oz) butter or margarine
25 g (1 oz) Cheddar cheese, grated

Whisk the egg white until stiff. In a separate bowl, beat the egg yolk, 15 ml (1 tbsp) water and salt and pepper together. Using a metal spoon, carefully fold the egg white into the yolk mixture. Melt the fat in a small, heavy-based frying pan and pour in the egg mixture. Cook over a low heat until the underside is set and lightly browned. Sprinkle with the cheese and place under a hot grill until the cheese has melted. Fold across the centre, invert on to a heated serving dish and serve immediately.

Serves 1   240 Calories (1010 kJ)
■△

Mediterranean omelette

15 g ($\frac{1}{2}$ oz) butter or margarine
1 small onion, skinned and finely chopped
1 garlic clove, skinned and crushed
100 g (4 oz) mushrooms, sliced
2 tomatoes, skinned and sliced
2 eggs
120 ml (8 tbsp) low-fat skimmed milk
salt and freshly ground pepper

Melt the fat in a non-stick omelette pan and sauté the onion for about 5 minutes until transparent but not coloured. Add the garlic and mushrooms and cook for 2–3 minutes, then add the tomatoes.

Beat the eggs, milk and salt and pepper together. Pour over the vegetable mixture and cook over a low heat until set. Serve cut in wedges.

Serves 2   195 Calories (810 kJ)
■△   per portion

Spanish omelette

Any cooked leftover vegetables may be used in this omelette. Serve with a salad or hot, lightly-buttered toast.

15 ml (1 tbsp) corn oil
1 onion, skinned and chopped
2 tomatoes, skinned and chopped
1 green pepper, seeded and chopped
1 red pepper, seeded and chopped
4 eggs
salt and freshly ground pepper

Heat the oil in a pan and sauté the onion for about 5 minutes until transparent. Add the tomatoes and peppers and continue cooking for a further 2–3 minutes. Beat the eggs with some salt and pepper and pour over the vegetable mixture. Cook over a low heat until the eggs are beginning to set and the base is golden brown. Place under a medium grill to cook the top. Serve cut in wedges.

Serves 4   130 Calories (550 kJ)
■△   per portion

Macaroni cheese

Serve this delicious family favourite with a salad or grilled tomatoes.

175 g (6 oz) short cut macaroni
40 g (1$\frac{1}{2}$ oz) butter or margarine
60 ml (4 level tbsp) flour
600 ml (1 pint) low-fat skimmed milk
salt and freshly ground pepper
pinch of grated nutmeg or 2.5 ml ($\frac{1}{2}$ level tsp) prepared mustard
175 g (6 oz) mature Cheddar cheese, grated

Cook the macaroni in boiling salted water for 10 minutes, then drain well. Meanwhile, melt the fat in a pan and add the flour. Cook for 2 minutes, stirring. Remove the pan from the heat and gradually stir in the milk. Bring to the boil and cook for 2 minutes, stirring continuously. Add the seasonings, 100 g (4 oz) of the cheese and the macaroni. Pour into an ovenproof dish and sprinkle with the remaining cheese. Bake in the oven at 200°C (400°F) mark 6 for about 20 minutes until golden and bubbling.

Serves 4   460 Calories (1920 kJ)
■△   per portion

VEGETABLES & SALADS

Dutch hussar's salad

350 g (12 oz) cold lean meat, eg. ham or chicken, diced
1 small cucumber, diced
3 eating apples, cored and diced
2 75-g (3-oz) cold, cooked potatoes, diced
1 lettuce, washed

For the cheese dressing

100 g (4 oz) cottage cheese
juice of $\frac{1}{2}$ a lemon
salt and freshly ground pepper

To garnish

2 hard-boiled eggs, sliced
1 cooked medium beetroot, skinned and diced
pickled onions or gherkins
3 tomatoes, skinned and sliced

Put the meat, cucumber, apples and potatoes in a bowl. For the dressing, combine together the cottage cheese, lemon juice and salt and pepper. Beat well until smooth and creamy, then add to the salad and toss lightly. Press the meat mixture into a 1.7-litre (3-pint) basin and leave in the refrigerator until well chilled.

Arrange some lettuce leaves on a serving dish and unmould the meat shape on to the lettuce. Garnish with hard-boiled egg slices, beetroot, pickled onions or gherkin fans and tomato slices. Serve with lightly buttered crispbread or crusty wholemeal bread.

Serves 4   280 Calories (1180 kJ)
■△△   *per portion*

Courgettes and tomatoes au gratin

Serve this light vegetable dish for supper with hot or cold sliced meat or grilled fish as a main course.

450 g (1 lb) courgettes, trimmed
salt and freshly ground pepper
425-g (15-oz) can tomatoes, drained
5 ml (1 level tsp) fines herbes
3 50-g (2-oz) tomatoes, skinned, seeded and chopped
5 ml (1 level tsp) mustard powder
150 ml ($\frac{1}{4}$ pint) natural yogurt
175 g (6 oz) Gouda cheese, grated
1 egg yolk

Cut the courgettes into 0.5-cm ($\frac{1}{4}$-inch) slices. Cook in boiling salted water for about 8 minutes until tender. Drain very well and keep warm. Place the canned tomatoes in a pan, add the herbs and boil uncovered to a thick pulp. Remove from the heat and add the chopped tomatoes.

Cream the mustard with 5 ml (1 tsp) water. Beat the yogurt, half the cheese, the egg yolk, salt and pepper and mustard together then cook gently until the mixture thickens. Arrange two rows of courgettes around the edge of a heated 1-litre (1$\frac{1}{2}$-pint) flameproof dish. Fill the base with half the remainder and season well. Add 40 g (1$\frac{1}{2}$ oz) cheese in an even layer. Top with the rest of the courgettes. Season, add the remaining cheese and top with the tomato sauce.

Pour about half the yogurt sauce over the tomatoes. Place under the grill to heat through and brown the topping. Serve the extra sauce with each portion.

Serves 4   205 Calories (865 kJ)
■△   *per portion*

Red cabbage and beetroot salad

An unusual, colourful salad to serve with a pork, lamb or fish dish.

275 g (10 oz) red cabbage, shredded
225 g (8 oz) cooked beetroot, skinned and diced
50 g (2 oz) onion, skinned and finely chopped
30 ml (2 tbsp) oil
15–30 ml (1–2 tbsp) red wine vinegar
salt and freshly ground pepper

In a salad bowl, toss together the cabbage, beetroot and onion. Combine the oil, vinegar, salt and pepper, shake together in a screw-topped jar or whisk with a fork. Pour the dressing over the salad and toss lightly. Leave for 30 minutes before serving.

Serves 6   70 Calories (290 kJ)
■△   per portion

Mushroom flan

For a well-balanced meal, serve this slimline vegetable flan with a salad such as Dressed courgette and leek salad (see page 106).

100 g (4 oz) wholemeal breadcrumbs
300 ml (½ pint) natural yogurt
salt and freshly ground pepper
4 eggs
150 ml (¼ pint) low-fat skimmed milk
175 g (6 oz) mushrooms, sliced
4 spring onions, chopped
75 g (3 oz) Cheddar cheese, grated

Mix together the breadcrumbs, half the yogurt and salt and pepper to form a paste. Use to line a 23-cm (9-inch) flan dish, pressing the paste into shape with the fingers.

Whisk the eggs, remaining yogurt and milk together, and season well. Place the mushrooms, onions and half the cheese on the base of the flan. Pour the egg mixture over the top and then sprinkle on the rest of the grated cheese. Bake in the oven at 180°C (350°F) mark 4 for about 30 minutes until brown and set. Serve warm.

Serves 4   300 Calories (1260 kJ)
■△   per portion

Cucumber salad

A refreshing side salad to serve with spicy foods.

2.5 ml (½ level tsp) Dijon mustard
2.5 ml (½ tsp) lemon juice
salt and freshly ground pepper
15 ml (1 tbsp) white wine vinegar
5 ml (1 tsp) Worcestershire sauce
10 ml (2 level tsp) dried chives
30 ml (2 tbsp) natural yogurt
225 g (8 oz) tomatoes, skinned, seeded and diced
350 g (12 oz) cucumber

In a bowl, whisk together the mustard, lemon juice, salt, pepper, vinegar, Worcestershire sauce, chives and yogurt. Fold in the tomato.

Meanwhile, wipe the cucumber and run a fork down the length to serrate, then slice thinly. Toss with the dressing and leave to marinate for about 1 hour.

Serves 4   30 Calories (120 kJ)
□△   per portion

Brazilian salad

Delicious served with cold pork or ham.

225 g (8 oz) tomatoes, skinned and sliced

1 celery heart, chopped

100 g (4 oz) fresh pineapple, chopped
or 226-g (8-oz) can unsweetened
pineapple pieces, drained

1 lettuce heart, washed

juice of 1 lemon

15 ml (1 tbsp) natural yogurt

a little cayenne pepper

Mix the tomatoes and celery with the pineapple pieces. Shred the lettuce heart and add
to the tomato mixture. Place in a serving
dish. Combine the lemon juice, yogurt and
cayenne pepper and spoon over the salad.

Serves 4   40 Calories (160 kJ)
□△△   per portion

Cauliflower niçoise

This new way to serve cauliflower compli-
ments all meat and fish dishes.

1 cauliflower

15 ml (1 tbsp) corn oil

1 small onion, skinned and chopped

1–2 garlic cloves, skinned and crushed

3 tomatoes, skinned and quartered

juice and finely grated rind of 1 lemon

Divide the cauliflower into florets and cook
in boiling salted water for 5 minutes. Drain,
place in a heated serving dish and keep hot.
Heat the oil in a pan and sauté the onion and
garlic. Add the tomatoes and cook for 3

minutes. Add the lemon juice and cook for a
further 2 minutes. Pour over the cauliflower
and serve sprinkled with grated lemon rind.

Serves 4   50 Calories (220 kJ)
□△△   per portion

Mixed salad platter

For a balanced menu, serve Watercress soup
(see page 48) before this main course salad
and Blackberry whip (see page 115) for
dessert.

450 g (1 lb) cottage cheese

2 peaches, skinned and sliced

juice of $\frac{1}{2}$ a lemon

275 g (10 oz) lean cooked ham,
sliced and rolled

50 g (2 oz) French beans,
topped and tailed

2 courgettes, trimmed and sliced

50 g (2 oz) mushrooms, sliced

1 green pepper, seeded and sliced

1 red pepper, seeded and sliced

2 cooked beetroots, skinned and diced

2 tomatoes, sliced

spring onions, trimmed

radishes, trimmed

Pile the cottage cheese into the centre of a
serving platter. Immerse the peach slices in
lemon juice, then drain. Arrange with the
ham rolls around the cheese. Blanch the
beans, courgettes and mushrooms in boiling salted water for 2 minutes. Drain well
and chill. Arrange decoratively with the
peppers, beetroot, tomatoes, spring onions
and radishes around the platter.

Serves 4   250 Calories (1050 kJ)
□△△   per portion

Cheese and tuna quiche (page 93)

Pasta prawn salad

Illustrated in colour opposite

If liked, about 30 ml (2 tbsp) oil and vinegar dressing may be stirred into this salad.

225 g (8 oz) small wholewheat pasta shapes
salt and freshly ground pepper
225 g (8 oz) peeled prawns
1 red or green pepper, seeded and chopped
225 g (8 oz) tomatoes, chopped

Cook the pasta in boiling salted water for 10 minutes until tender. Drain, rinse with cold water and drain again. Place in a salad bowl and add the prawns, pepper and tomatoes. Season to taste, mix well together and serve.

Serves 6   190 Calories (805 kJ)
□△△   per portion

Cauliflower and tuna salad

Serve with lightly buttered wholemeal toast or Melba toast.

225-g (8-oz) head cauliflower, trimmed
150 ml ($\frac{1}{4}$ pint) natural yogurt
15 ml (1 tbsp) snipped fresh chives
1.25 ml ($\frac{1}{4}$ level tsp) mustard powder
1 small garlic clove, skinned and crushed
5 ml (1 tsp) lemon juice
salt and freshly ground pepper
198-g (7-oz) can tuna, drained and flaked
1 red eating apple, cored and diced
lettuce leaves, washed

Divide the cauliflower into tiny florets. Blanch in boiling salted water for 2 minutes. Drain and plunge into cold water, then drain again.

In a bowl, combine the yogurt, chives, mustard, garlic, lemon juice and salt and pepper to taste. Fold through the cauliflower, tuna and apple. Divide between two lettuce lined plates.

Serves 2   285 Calories (1190 kJ)
□△△   per portion

Wholewheat salad

Illustrated in colour opposite

Nutritious wheat is an ideal base for a salad. It is slightly chewy with a nutty flavour.

225 g (8 oz) wholewheat grain
3 sticks of celery, sliced
$\frac{1}{2}$ cucumber, diced
45 ml (3 tbsp) sunflower oil
30 ml (2 tbsp) white wine vinegar
15 ml (1 level tbsp) whole grain mustard
salt and freshly ground pepper

Soak the wholewheat for at least 2 hours or overnight in plenty of cold water. Drain, place in a large pan of boiling water and simmer for 25 minutes until the grains have a little bite left. Drain, rinse with cold water and drain again. Place in a bowl with the celery and cucumber.

Mix the oil and vinegar together with the mustard and plenty of seasoning. Pour over the salad and toss together. Chill for several hours before serving. Stir again just before serving.

Serves 6   165 Calories (690 kJ)
■△   per portion

Clockwise from top: Pasta prawn salad (*above*), Green beans Sorrento (*page 107*), Wholewheat salad (*above*)

Lemony peas and celery

This delicious vegetable accompaniment is simple to prepare and high in fibre. Serve with any fish or meat dish.

25 g (1 oz) butter or margarine
4 sticks of celery, thinly sliced
350 g (12 oz) fresh or frozen peas
10 ml (2 tsp) lemon juice
salt and freshly ground pepper

Melt the butter or margarine in a pan and sauté the celery for 5 minutes. Add the peas, lemon juice and salt and pepper. Cover and cook over a low heat until the peas are cooked.

Serves 4   110 Calories (460 kJ)
■△△   per portion

Spinach salad

For a complete meal, serve this interesting salad with hard-boiled eggs.

225 g (8 oz) young spinach, washed
8 streaky bacon rashers, rinded and chopped
2 slices of wholemeal bread
30 ml (2 tbsp) corn oil
15 ml (1 tbsp) lemon juice
salt and freshly ground pepper

Shred the spinach, discarding any tough stems, into small strips. Fry the bacon in its own fat for about 5 minutes until crisp and golden brown. Remove from the pan and drain on absorbent kitchen paper. Toast the bread until golden brown and cut into 1-cm ($\frac{1}{2}$-inch) cubes.

Whisk the oil, lemon juice and salt and pepper together. Toss the spinach in the dressing and scatter the croûtons and bacon on top.

Serves 4   300 Calories (1265 kJ)
■△   per portion

Italian peppers

Serve as a light lunch with brown rice or alone as a starter.

2 175-g (6-oz) green or red peppers
15 ml (1 tbsp) corn oil
100 g (4 oz) courgettes, trimmed and diced
150 g (5 oz) aubergine, skinned and chopped
3 tomatoes, skinned and roughly chopped
50 g (2 oz) lean ham, finely chopped
1 garlic clove, skinned and crushed
2.5 ml ($\frac{1}{2}$ level tsp) dried oregano
salt and freshly ground pepper
chicken stock

Cut the peppers in half lengthways and discard the seeds. Heat the oil in a pan and sauté the courgettes, aubergine and tomatoes until they start to break down. Add the ham, garlic and oregano. Season well. Use to stuff the pepper halves. Arrange in a baking dish with a little stock. Cover and cook in the oven at 180°C (350°F) mark 4 for about 45 minutes until the peppers are tender but still crisp. Allow to cool before serving but do not refrigerate.

Serves 2   90 Calories (375 kJ)
□△△   per portion

Dressed broccoli

An ideal summer vegetable dish to serve with cold meats or fish.

100 g (4 oz) frozen sweetcorn kernels
100 g (4 oz) broccoli spears
salt and freshly ground pepper
100 g (4 oz) firm ripe tomatoes, skinned, seeded and diced

For the dressing

45 ml (3 tbsp) white wine vinegar
45 ml (3 tbsp) lemon juice
15 ml (1 tbsp) corn oil
2.5 ml ($\frac{1}{2}$ level tsp) mustard powder
15 ml (1 tbsp) snipped fresh chives or chopped spring onion

Cook the sweetcorn as directed on the packet. Divide the broccoli into small florets. Cook the broccoli in boiling salted water for about 10 minutes until tender but still crisp and bright green. Drain and refresh in cold water. Drain again and mix with the sweetcorn.

Place the dressing ingredients in a screw-topped jar and shake well to combine. Season to taste, pour over the tomatoes, then spoon over the broccoli and sweetcorn. Leave for 30 minutes, turning the vegetables occasionally, before serving.

Serves 2   145 Calories (610 kJ)
■△△   *per portion*

White fish salad bowl

If preferred, any other white fish may be used in this salad instead of cod or dogfish.

225 g (8 oz) cod or dogfish fillet, skinned
1 bay leaf
1.25 ml ($\frac{1}{4}$ level tsp) fennel seeds
salt and freshly ground pepper
150 ml ($\frac{1}{4}$ pint) natural yogurt
5 ml (1 level tsp) French mustard
small piece garlic clove, skinned and crushed
1 small lettuce, washed
2 sticks of celery, finely chopped
3 spring onions, chopped
2 tomatoes, skinned, seeded and chopped, to garnish

Place the fish in a pan and cover with water. Add the bay leaf, fennel seeds and salt and pepper. Cover and poach for about 10 minutes. Drain the fish and cool.

Combine the yogurt, mustard and garlic and season to taste. Line a serving dish with the lettuce. Pile the flaked fish in the centre and sprinkle the celery and onion on top. Spoon over the yogurt dressing and garnish with tomato.

Serves 2   170 Calories (710 kJ)
□△   *per portion*

Aubergines à la Provençale

Serve this colourful, nutritious vegetable dish for supper with grilled meats.

2 aubergines

salt and freshly ground pepper

25 g (1 oz) butter or margarine

4 small tomatoes, skinned and chopped

1 shallot, skinned and chopped

1 onion, skinned and chopped

50 g (2 oz) fresh wholemeal breadcrumbs

50 g (2 oz) Cheddar cheese, grated

parsley sprigs to garnish

Do not peel the aubergines, but wipe them and steam or boil for about 30 minutes. When tender, drain them and cut in half lengthways. Scoop out the flesh, chop and season. Reserve the aubergine skins.

Heat the fat in a pan and sauté the chopped tomatoes, shallot and onion. Add the aubergine flesh and a few breadcrumbs. Fill the aubergine shells with this mixture, sprinkle with the remaining breadcrumbs and then with the grated cheese. Place under the grill and cook until golden brown on top. Serve garnished with parsley.

Serves 4   175 Calories (730 kJ)
■△△△   *per portion*

Dressed courgette and leek salad

350 g (12 oz) courgettes, trimmed

275 g (10 oz) leeks, washed and sliced

For the dressing

30 ml (2 tbsp) corn oil

15 ml (1 tbsp) distilled vinegar

1.25 ml ($\frac{1}{4}$ level tsp) dried oregano or marjoram

1.25 ml ($\frac{1}{4}$ level tsp) dried mixed herbs

1.25 ml ($\frac{1}{4}$ level tsp) onion salt

2.5 ml ($\frac{1}{2}$ level tsp) chopped fresh chives

salt and freshly ground pepper

In a screw-topped jar, combine the oil, vinegar, herbs, onion salt, chives and salt and pepper. Shake well, then leave to infuse for 30 minutes.

Cut the courgettes into 0.5-cm ($\frac{1}{4}$-inch) slices. Blanch in boiling water for a few minutes until tender but still crisp. Drain and pat dry with absorbent kitchen paper. Blanch the leeks in boiling water for about 2 minutes. Drain well and add to the courgettes. Shake the dressing until creamy and pour over the vegetables whilst still warm. Toss lightly, then chill before serving.

Serves 4   100 Calories (420 kJ)
■△   *per portion*

Tomato and onion bake

A simple vegetable casserole.

3–4 onions, skinned and sliced

3–4 tomatoes, sliced

salt and freshly ground pepper

25 g (1 oz) butter

Place alternate layers of onion and tomato in an ovenproof dish. Sprinkle with salt and pepper and dot with the butter. Cover and bake in the oven at 180°C (350°F) mark 4 for 30–45 minutes until tender.

Serves 3–4   85–115 Calories
□△   (360–475 kJ) per portion

Baked courgettes and aubergines

A colourful vegetable accompaniment, particularly good with lamb.

olive oil

2 aubergines, sliced

salt and freshly ground pepper

6–8 shallots, skinned and sliced

1 garlic clove, skinned and chopped

6–7 courgettes, trimmed and sliced

45 ml (3 level tbsp) tomato purée

150 ml ($\frac{1}{4}$ pint) chicken stock

olives to garnish

Rub an ovenproof dish lightly with oil. Put a layer of aubergine in the bottom, and sprinkle with salt and pepper. Cover with a layer of shallot and a little garlic, then a layer of courgettes. Continue the layers until the dish is filled.

Mix together the tomato purée and stock and pour over the vegetables. Bake in the oven at 180°C (350°F) mark 4 for 1 hour until the vegetables are tender. Serve hot or cold, garnished with a few olives.

Serves 4   65 Calories (270 kJ)
□△△   per portion

Green beans Sorrento

Illustrated in colour on page 102

An exciting vegetable dish to serve with grilled meat or fish. Use fresh beans when in season, if preferred.

25 g (1 oz) bacon, rinded and chopped

50 g (2 oz) onion, skinned and finely chopped

1 garlic clove, skinned and chopped

50 g (2 oz) green pepper, seeded and finely chopped

1 medium tomato, chopped

454-g (1-lb) packet frozen haricots verts

2.5 ml ($\frac{1}{2}$ level tsp) oregano

salt and freshly ground pepper

Sauté the bacon in a pan in its own fat until lightly browned. Add the onion, garlic and green pepper and sauté until golden brown. Stir in the tomato, beans, oregano, salt, pepper and 60 ml (4 tbsp) water. Bring to the boil, cover and simmer for about 10 minutes, until the beans are tender. Serve immediately.

Serves 4   50 Calories (210 kJ)
□△   per portion

Dressed French beans

450 g (1 lb) French beans, trimmed

salt and freshly ground pepper

1.25 ml ($\frac{1}{4}$ level tsp) mustard powder

30 ml (2 tbsp) salad oil

15 ml (1 tbsp) tarragon or
white wine vinegar

Cook the beans in boiling salted water for 10–15 minutes until tender. Drain well, season and allow to cool. Blend the mustard, oil and vinegar together. Toss the cooled French beans in this dressing.

Serves 4   70 Calories (290 kJ)
◼△   per portion

Stuffed tomatoes

Instead of breadcrumbs, try 25 g (1 oz) cooked brown rice in the filling.

4 large tomatoes

7 g ($\frac{1}{4}$ oz) butter

25 g (1 oz) cooked ham, chopped

5 ml (1 tsp) chopped onion

30 ml (2 level tbsp) fresh wholemeal
breadcrumbs

2.5 ml ($\frac{1}{2}$ tsp) chopped fresh parsley

salt and freshly ground pepper

30 ml (2 level tbsp) Cheddar cheese,
grated (optional)

Cut a small round from each tomato at the end opposite to the stalk. Scoop out the centres and reserve. Melt the butter in a pan and lightly fry the ham and onion for 3 minutes. Add the breadcrumbs, parsley, salt and pepper, cheese (if used) and the pulp removed from the tomatoes. Fill the tomatoes with this mixture, pile it neatly on top and put on the lids. Bake in the oven at 200°C (400°F) mark 6 for 10–15 minutes.

Serves 4   85 Calories (360 kJ)
□△   per portion

Stuffed peppers

4 green peppers, halved lengthways
and seeded

40 g ($1\frac{1}{2}$ oz) butter

1 onion, skinned and chopped

100 g (4 oz) bacon, rinded and chopped

4 tomatoes, skinned and sliced

100 g (4 oz) cooked long-grain rice

salt and freshly ground pepper

60 ml (4 level tbsp) grated
Cheddar cheese

50 g (2 oz) fresh wholemeal
breadcrumbs

150 ml ($\frac{1}{4}$ pint) chicken stock

Put the halved peppers in an ovenproof dish. Melt 25 g (1 oz) of the butter in a pan and lightly fry the onion and bacon until golden brown. Add the tomatoes, cooked rice, salt, pepper and half the cheese. Mix the rest of the cheese with the breadcrumbs. Put the bacon stuffing into the pepper cases and sprinkle with the breadcrumb mixture. Pour the stock round the peppers and top each with a knob of the remaining butter. Cook in the oven at 190°C (375°F) mark 5 for 15–20 minutes until cooked.

Serves 4   340 Calories (1430 kJ)
◼△   per portion

Leek and sprout salad

Try adding diced green pepper and celery to this versatile winter salad.

225 g (8 oz) Brussels sprouts, trimmed and very thinly sliced
175 g (6 oz) leeks, washed and thinly sliced
5 ml (1 level tsp) celery seeds
30 ml (2 tbsp) corn oil
30 ml (2 tbsp) distilled vinegar
salt and freshly ground pepper

Place the sliced Brussels sprouts in a salad bowl. Separate the leeks into rings and blanch in boiling water for 1–2 minutes. Drain and pat dry with absorbent kitchen paper. Add to the sprouts.

In a screw-topped jar, combine the celery seeds, oil, vinegar and salt and pepper. Shake well, pour over the vegetables and toss. Serve lightly chilled.

Serves 4   90 Calories (375 kJ)
■△   *per portion*

Pickled beetroot

Beetroot is a popular vegetable to serve with cold meats. It may be pickled in a vinegar dressing without the gelatine.

450 ml (¾ pint) water
20 ml (4 level tsp) powdered gelatine
150 ml (¼ pint) vinegar
few drops of liquid artificial sweetener
225 g (8 oz) cooked beetroot, skinned and sliced

Place the water in a bowl and put it in a pan of hot water. Sprinkle over the gelatine and leave to dissolve. Add the vinegar and artificial sweetener to the dissolved gelatine. Pour over the beetroot and leave to set.

Serves 4   25 Calories (110 kJ)
□△   *per portion*

Three-bean casserole

225 g (8 oz) French beans, trimmed
225 g (8 oz) medium parsnips, peeled and sliced
225 g (8 oz) onions, skinned and finely chopped
396-g (14-oz) can tomatoes
432-g (15-oz) can red kidney beans, drained
425-g (15-oz) can butter beans, drained
15 ml (1 tbsp) tomato relish
2.5 ml (½ tsp) Worcestershire sauce
salt and freshly ground pepper

Cut the French beans into three. Cook the parsnips in boiling salted water for about 15 minutes and, when nearly tender, add the French beans. Cook until both are tender, then drain well and separate the parsnips from the beans.

Put the onions in a pan with the tomatoes and their juice. Simmer gently until the onions are just soft. Add the kidney and butter beans, French beans, relish, Worcestershire sauce and salt and pepper. Transfer to a 1.4-litre (2½-pint) deep ovenproof dish. Layer the sliced cooked parsnips on top and cook in the oven at 190°C (375°F) mark 5 for about 35 minutes.

Serves 4   215 Calories (900 kJ)
□△△△   *per portion*

Stuffed baked onions

4 225-g (8-oz) onions, skinned

100 g (4 oz) cooked chicken meat

100 g (4 oz) cooked ham

$\frac{1}{4}$ small green pepper, seeded

2.5 ml ($\frac{1}{2}$ level tsp) dried marjoram

salt and freshly ground pepper

150 ml ($\frac{1}{4}$ pint) natural yogurt

5 ml (1 level tsp) mustard

1 egg

chopped fresh parsley to garnish

Halve the onions from stalk to root. Remove the centre segments and reserve. Blanch the halves in boiling salted water for 10 minutes, then drain thoroughly. Mince together the reserved onion centres, the chicken, ham, and green pepper. Season with the marjoram, salt and pepper.

Place the onions, cut side up, in a large shallow casserole and fill the hollows with the chicken mixture. Cover and bake in the oven at 190°C (375°F) mark 5 for about 45 minutes.

Beat together the yogurt, mustard and egg. Coat each onion with the yogurt mixture. Return to the oven, uncovered, and bake for a further 20 minutes, for the topping to set. Garnish with the parsley.

Serves 4   160 Calories (670 kJ)
□△   *per portion*

Baked beef-stuffed marrow

1–2 small marrows (total weight about 1.4 kg/3 lb)

15 ml (1 tbsp) corn oil

350 g (12 oz) lean minced beef

75 g (3 oz) onion, skinned and chopped

25 g (1 oz) fresh wholemeal breadcrumbs

1 egg, beaten

salt and freshly ground pepper

2.5 ml ($\frac{1}{2}$ level tsp) dried oregano

450 g (1 lb) tomatoes, sliced

watercress sprigs to garnish

Cut the marrow(s) in half lengthways and scoop out the seeds. Do not peel. Heat the oil in a pan and fry the minced beef. Add the onion and fry gently. Leave to cool slightly then bind with the breadcrumbs and beaten egg. Season well with salt, pepper and oregano.

Fill the marrow with the meat mixture, top with the sliced tomatoes and season again. Place in an ovenproof dish, cover and bake in the oven at 190°C (375°F) mark 5 for about 45 minutes. Garnish with watercress.

Serves 4   240 Calories (1005 kJ)
■△△   *per portion*

Cottage cheese baked potatoes

Popular with all the family, try a different filling in this tasty supper dish, such as 100 g (4 oz) cottage cheese with chives.

2 175-g (6-oz) potatoes
50 g (2 oz) cooked ham, chopped
225 g (8 oz) cottage cheese
salt and freshly ground pepper
5 ml (1 level tsp) mustard
watercress sprigs to garnish

Scrub the potatoes and prick with a fork. Bake in the oven at 200°C (400°F) mark 6 about 1 hour until tender. Cut in half and scoop out the potato. Mix with the ham, cottage cheese, salt, pepper and mustard. Pile back into the potato shells and reheat in the oven for 5 minutes. Serve garnished with watercress.

Serves 2   295 Calories (1235 kJ)
■△   per portion

Dijon potatoes

This tasty new way to serve potatoes is delicious served with roast meat.

1 kg (2 lb) potatoes, peeled and thinly sliced
2 large onions, skinned and thinly sliced
30 ml (2 tbsp) chopped fresh chives
30 ml (2 level tbsp) Dijon mustard
300 ml ($\frac{1}{2}$ pint) chicken stock
salt and freshly ground pepper
25 g (1 oz) butter, melted

Arrange the potatoes and onions in alternate layers in a casserole, sprinkling each layer with the chives and ending with a potato layer. Blend together the mustard, stock and salt and pepper and pour over the potatoes and onions. Brush the melted butter over the top. Cover and bake in the oven at 180°C (350°F) mark 4 for 2 hours. Cook uncovered for the final 30 minutes to brown the top before serving.

Serves 6   185 Calories (780 kJ)
□△△   per portion

Celery salad in yogurt dressing

This versatile salad is excellent served with thick slices of lean cooked meat, eg. ham, or flaked tuna fish.

1 head of celery, trimmed and chopped
150 ml ($\frac{1}{4}$ pint) natural yogurt
grated rind of 1 lemon
15 ml (1 tbsp) lemon juice
5 ml (1 level tsp) caster sugar
15 ml (1 level tbsp) chopped fresh mint
salt and freshly ground pepper
4 walnut halves, chopped
mint leaves to garnish

Place the celery in a bowl with the yogurt, lemon rind and juice, caster sugar, chopped mint and salt and pepper. Mix well. Transfer to a serving dish, cover and chill in the refrigerator until needed.

Just before serving, fold in the nuts and garnish with mint leaves.

Serves 4   80 Calories (325 kJ)
□△   per portion

SLIM & FIT FAMILY COOK BOOK

Ham and cheese salad

A quick-to-prepare main course salad for busy days. For a well-balanced meal, serve with soup and a dessert prepared in advance, such as Banana crush (see page 124).

1 stick of celery, diced
1 spring onion, finely chopped
100 g (4 oz) cottage cheese
2 tomatoes, sliced
1 hard-boiled egg, sliced
1 slice of boiled ham, cut 2.5 cm (1 inch) thick and diced

Mix the celery, onion and cottage cheese together. Pile in the centre of a serving dish. Arrange the tomatoes, hard-boiled egg and diced ham around the edges.

Serves 2   230 Calories (960 kJ)
■△   *per portion*

Crunchy salad

A crisp salad, suitable as a main course for a light lunch or supper dish. Serve with warm, crusty bread.

2 eating apples, cored and roughly chopped
15 ml (1 tbsp) lemon juice
100 g (4 oz) Cheddar cheese, diced
2 sticks of celery, sliced
25 g (1 oz) walnuts, chopped
225 g (8 oz) white cabbage, shredded
150 ml ($\frac{1}{4}$ pint) natural yogurt
chopped fresh parsley to garnish

Toss the apple in the lemon juice and place in a salad bowl. Add the diced cheese, celery, walnuts and cabbage and mix together. Pour the yogurt over the salad and toss well. Sprinkle with parsley and serve.

Serves 4   210 Calories (870 kJ)
■△   *per portion*

Ratatouille

Serve this colourful vegetable dish as a vegetable accompaniment, starter or with nutty wholemeal bread for supper.

2 large onions, skinned and sliced
1 large aubergine, chopped
4 tomatoes, skinned and chopped
4 courgettes, trimmed and sliced
1 green or red pepper, seeded and sliced
1 garlic clove, skinned and crushed
30 ml (2 level tbsp) tomato purée
salt and freshly ground pepper
chopped fresh parsley to garnish

Place the prepared vegetables, garlic, tomato purée, and salt and pepper in a casserole. Stir well and cover tightly. Cook in the oven at 180°C (350°F) mark 4 for 1–1$\frac{1}{4}$ hours until all the vegetables are tender. Serve garnished with parsley.

Serves 4   80 Calories (335 kJ)
□△△   *per portion*

PUDDINGS & DESSERTS

Coconut fruit crisp

Comice or William pears are the best choice for this pudding.

2 egg yolks

150-g (5-oz) carton pear yogurt

4 ripe pears, peeled, cored and roughly chopped

25 g (1 oz) desiccated coconut

Blend the egg yolks with the yogurt in a bowl and stir in the chopped pears. Place the mixture in an 18-cm (7-inch) ovenproof dish. Bake in the oven at 180°C (350°F) mark 4 for 30 minutes until set. A few minutes before removing from the oven, sprinkle coconut over the pudding.

Serves 4   150 Calories (625 kJ)
■△△   per portion

Date-filled oranges

For this unusual baked orange dessert, choose oranges that are heavy for their size as these generally have a better ratio of flesh to pith.

4 large oranges

1 lemon

150 ml ($\frac{1}{4}$ pint) hot water

100 g (4 oz) fresh dates, stoned and chopped

25 g (1 oz) walnut pieces, chopped

30 ml (2 tbsp) clear honey

pinch of ground cinnamon

Using a potato peeler, thinly pare the oranges and lemon. Put the parings in a bowl and pour over the hot water. Leave to infuse.

Remove all traces of white pith from the oranges with a serrated knife and remove their centres with a sharp knife or apple corer. Add any juice to the bowl with the pared rind and the juice of the lemon. Mix the dates and walnuts together and use to fill the centre of each orange.

Strain the fruit juices into a pan. Add the honey and cinnamon and bring to the boil. Place the oranges in an ovenproof dish just large enough to take the four in a single layer. Pour over the honeyed juices. Cook in the oven at 190°C (375°F) mark 5 for 15 minutes. Serve hot.

Serves 4   125 Calories (525 kJ)
□△△   per portion

Spiced fruit pudding

A satisfying pudding to serve after a light main course. White fish salad bowl (see page 105) and a soup to start would make a perfectly balanced menu.

75 g (3 oz) fresh breadcrumbs

2 eggs, separated

300 ml ($\frac{1}{2}$ pint) low-fat skimmed milk

7.5 ml ($1\frac{1}{2}$ level tsp) ground mixed spice

25 g (1 oz) dried fruit

Place the breadcrumbs in a 1.1-litre (2-pint) ovenproof dish. Beat the egg yolks with the milk and stir in the mixed spice. Pour this over the breadcrumbs, add the dried fruit and mix well together. Leave to stand for 20 minutes.

Whisk the egg whites until stiff and gently fold into the bread mixture. Cook in the oven at 180°C (350°F) mark 4 for 40 minutes until golden brown.

Serves 4   130 Calories (545 kJ)
□△   per portion

Gingered apple crunch

Sprinkle a little caster sugar over the apples, if liked.

450 g (1 lb) cooking apples, peeled, cored and sliced
2.5 ml (½ level tsp) ground ginger
100 ml (4 fl oz) low-calorie ginger ale
75 g (3 oz) muesli

Place the apple slices in a 1.1-litre (2-pint) ovenproof dish. Sprinkle with the ground ginger and pour over the ginger ale. Cover with the muesli. Cook in the oven at 180°C (350°F) mark 4 for 30 minutes until golden.

Serves 4   110 Calories (465 kJ)
□△   per portion

Banana and hazelnut fool

350 g (12 oz) bananas
25 g (1 oz) soft dark brown sugar
150-g (5-oz) carton hazelnut yogurt
7.5 ml (1½ level tsp) powdered gelatine
1 egg white
whole toasted hazelnuts and angelica to decorate

Peel and mash the bananas and blend with the brown sugar until smooth. Combine with the yogurt. Put 30 ml (2 tbsp) water in a cup and place in a pan of hot water. Sprinkle the gelatine into the cup and heat very gently until dissolved. Add the dissolved gelatine to the banana mixture. Whisk the egg white until stiff but not dry and fold into the banana mixture with a metal spoon. Spoon into four individual glasses. Cover and chill quickly. Decorate each dessert with a whole hazelnut and angelica leaves. Serve at once.

Serves 4   115 Calories (475 kJ)
□△   per portion

Blackberry whip

A colourful dessert which is economical to make in the autumn, when cooking apples are in season, and you can pick your own blackberries.

450 g (1 lb) blackberries
225 g (8 oz) cooking apples, peeled, cored and sliced
150 ml (¼ pint) water
15 ml (3 level tsp) powdered gelatine
liquid artificial sweetener to taste
2 egg whites
25 g (1 oz) desiccated coconut to decorate

Cook the blackberries and apples in the water until tender, then press through a sieve. Put 45 ml (3 tbsp) water in a cup and place in a pan of hot water. Sprinkle the gelatine into the cup and heat very gently until dissolved. Add the gelatine water and artificial sweetener to taste to the fruit purée. Leave the mixture to cool and thicken, but do not allow to set.

Whisk the egg whites until stiff, then fold carefully into the mixture. Pour into individual glasses and sprinkle with coconut. Chill before serving.

Serves 4   120 Calories (500 kJ)
□△△△   per portion

Apricot and pineapple whip

Ripe apricots are needed in this recipe. Test them for ripeness by pressing very gently. If ripe, they will yield to the light pressure.

1 kg (2 lb) fresh ripe apricots, halved and stoned

900 ml (1½ pints) unsweetened pineapple juice

30 ml (2 level tbsp) powdered gelatine

Simmer the apricots in the pineapple juice until tender, then chill well. Press through a sieve or liquidise in a blender to combine thoroughly.

Put 60 ml (4 tbsp) water in a cup and place in a pan of hot water. Sprinkle the gelatine into the cup and heat very gently until dissolved. Stir into the fruit mixture. Pour into eight glasses and leave to set.

Serves 8   70 Calories (290 kJ)
□△△   per portion

Spanish cream

In summer, serve with soft fruits such as strawberries.

600 ml (1 pint) low-fat skimmed milk

15 ml (3 level tsp) powdered gelatine

3 eggs, separated

artificial sweetener to taste

2.5 ml (½ tsp) vanilla flavouring

Put 30 ml (2 tbsp) of the milk in a cup and place in a pan of hot water. Sprinkle the gelatine into the cup and heat very gently until dissolved. Lightly beat the egg yolks with the remaining milk and heat gently without boiling, stirring continuously. Remove from the heat and add the gelatine mixture, aritifical sweetener to taste and vanilla flavouring. Mix thoroughly, then cool. Beat the egg whites until stiff and fold carefully into the custard with a metal spoon. Pour the mixture into four glasses and leave to set.

Serves 4   115 Calories (485 kJ)
□△   per portion

Oat-topped apples

700 g (1½ lb) cooking apples, peeled and cored

30 ml (2 tbsp) lemon juice

liquid artificial sweetener to taste

For the crumble topping

50 g (2 oz) butter or margarine

75 g (3 oz) plain flour

25 g (1 oz) rolled oats

25 g (1 oz) demerara sugar

2.5 ml (½ level tsp) ground mixed spice

Thinly slice the apples and put them in a greased ovenproof dish with the lemon juice and liquid sweetener.

For the topping, rub the fat into the flour until the mixture resembles fine breadcrumbs, then stir in the remaining ingredients. Spoon evenly over the apples. Bake in the oven at 180°C (350°F) mark 4 for 40–45 minutes until the apple is tender and the crumble is crisp and golden brown.

Serves 4–6   185–280 Calories
■△   (780–1170 kJ) per portion

Banana sherbet

This refreshingly light dessert is low in calories and, as well as being an ideal dinner dessert, is a favourite with children.

3 medium or 2 large bananas
150 ml ($\frac{1}{4}$ pint) lemon juice
600 ml (1 pint) unsweetened orange juice
300 ml ($\frac{1}{2}$ pint) low-fat skimmed milk
liquid artificial sweetener to taste
lemon or orange twists to decorate

Peel and mash the bananas and blend with the lemon juice. Add the orange juice and milk. Stir in artificial sweetener to taste. Turn the mixture into an empty ice cream container or into ice cube trays, and freeze for 1 hour.

Turn the mixture into a bowl and beat thoroughly until the ice crystals are broken down and the mixture is smooth. Return to the freezing containers and freeze until firm.

Spoon into four individual glass dishes and decorate with twists of lemon or orange.

Serves 4   *110 Calories (460 kJ)*
□△   *per portion*

Florida sponge pudding

A satisfying pudding without too many calories.

1 orange, peeled and segmented
1 grapefruit, peeled and segmented
2 eggs
25 g (1 oz) caster sugar
50 g (2 oz) plain flour

Lightly grease and flour an 18-cm (7-inch) sandwich tin. Arrange the fruit segments in the base of the tin. Put the eggs and sugar in a bowl placed over a pan of hot water and whisk until pale and thick. Remove from the heat and continue whisking until cool. Sift the flour on to the mixture and gently fold in with a metal spoon. Pour the sponge mixture over the fruit. Bake in the oven at 200°C (400°F) mark 6 for 10–15 minutes until golden and firm to the touch. Allow to cool, then turn out on to a serving plate.

Serves 4–6   *90–135 Calories*
□△   *(375–565 kJ) per portion*

Fresh orange custard

An attractive dessert, popular with children, combining tangy fruit and a creamy custard.

600 ml (1 pint) low-fat skimmed milk
2 150-g (5-oz) oranges
3 eggs
25 g (1 oz) caster sugar
grated nutmeg

Put the milk in a pan with the thinly pared rind of 1 orange. Heat gently but do not boil. Beat the eggs and sugar together and pour the warm milk over.

Strain the custard into a 1-litre (1½-pint) ovenproof dish and grate a little nutmeg over the top. Bake in the oven at 170°C (325°F) mark 3 for about 45 minutes until set. Allow to cool in the dish. Peel the oranges, removing all the white pith. Slice thinly and arrange in a circle around the edge of the custard.

Serves 4   160 Calories (675 kJ)
□△   per portion

Spiced pear crunch

A favourite with children, this dish combines natural flavours to make a delicious summer dessert.

450 g (1 lb) firm dessert pears, peeled, cored and sliced
150 ml (¼ pint) water
grated rind of ½ a lemon
small piece of cinnamon stick
liquid artificial sweetener to taste
50 g (2 oz) corn flakes
25 g (1 oz) butter

Place the pears, water, lemon rind and cinnamon in a pan and cook gently until the pears are tender. Remove the cinnamon stick. Lift the pears out of the juice and arrange them in a shallow flameproof serving dish. Add artificial sweetener to the juice to taste and spoon over the pears. Sprinkle with the corn flakes and dot with butter. Place the dish under a moderate grill for about 5 minutes, then serve immediately.

Serves 4   130 Calories (545 kJ)
□△   per portion

Frozen summer fruit sundae

If buttermilk is difficult to obtain, use natural yogurt in this sorbet dessert.

15 ml (3 level tsp) powdered gelatine
900 g (2 lb) soft fruit such as raspberries, strawberries or blackberries, sieved
2 eggs, separated
300 ml (½ pint) buttermilk
liquid artificial sweetener to taste

Put 45 ml (3 tbsp) water in a cup and place in a pan of hot water. Sprinkle the gelatine over the water and leave to dissolve. Add to the fruit pulp, with the beaten egg yolks and buttermilk. Add artificial sweetener to taste.

Pour into freezing containers or ice trays and freeze for 30 minutes until partially set. Turn out into a bowl and beat vigorously. Carefully fold in the whisked egg whites with a metal spoon. Return the mixture to the freezer trays and freeze. Serve in individual glasses.

Serves 6–8   55–75 Calories
□△△   (230–310 kJ) per portion

Apricot cheesecake (page 121)

PUDDINGS & DESSERTS

Lemon rise

A quick-to-prepare soufflé dessert which can also be made using grated orange rind.

---
4 eggs, separated

45 ml (3 level tbsp) icing sugar

grated rind of 1 lemon

Lightly grease and flour a 1.4-litre (2½-pint) ovenproof dish. Whisk the egg yolks, icing sugar and lemon rind until thick and creamy. Whisk the egg whites until stiff and fold into the egg yolk mixture. Put into the prepared dish. Cook in the oven at 190°C (375°F) mark 5 for 15–18 minutes until well risen and golden brown.

Serves 4   130 Calories (545 kJ)
■△   *per portion*

Rhubarb and almond compote

Adding natural yogurt turns stewed rhubarb into a creamy fool without the high fat content of cream.

---
450 g (1 lb) rhubarb, trimmed

150 ml (¼ pint) water

liquid artificial sweetener to taste

600 ml (1 pint) natural yogurt

toasted flaked almonds to decorate

Cut the rhubarb into 1-cm (½-inch) pieces and place in a pan with the water. Simmer gently until tender but not mushy. Add a little artificial sweetener to taste and leave to cool.

When the rhubarb is cool, stir in the yogurt, mixing well, and spoon into four individual glasses. Sprinkle a few toasted flaked almonds on top of each one before serving.

Serves 4   85 Calories (360 kJ)
□△   *per portion*

Apricot cheesecake

Illustrated in colour on page 119

Try canned unsweetened peaches or pineapple as an alternative topping.

220-g (8-oz) can apricot halves in natural juice, drained

2 eggs

25 g (1 oz) caster sugar

grated rind of 1 lemon

juice of ½ a lemon

100 g (4 oz) cottage cheese, sieved

150 ml (¼ pint) soured cream

15 g (½ oz) plain flour

Thoroughly dry the fruit on absorbent kitchen paper. Line the base of a 15-cm (6-inch) sandwich tin with silicone (non-stick) paper.

Beat the eggs lightly and add the remaining ingredients, mixing well. Pour into the prepared tin. Bake in the oven at 180°C (350°F) mark 4 for 30 minutes. Turn the oven off and leave the cheesecake in the oven until almost cool.

Carefully loosen the cheesecake from the sides of the tin with a knife and turn it out on to a warmed serving plate. Remove the lining paper and decorate the top of the cheesecake with the apricot halves. Serve the cheesecake while it is still warm.

Serves 6   195 Calories (820 kJ)
■△   *per portion*

Paella *(page 135)*

Walnut pear meringue

This versatile dessert is ideal to serve at a family meal or when entertaining.

4 ripe pears, peeled, halved and cored
25 g (1 oz) walnuts, chopped
4 glacé cherries, chopped
2 egg whites
25 g (1 oz) caster sugar

Place the pear halves, cut side up, in an oven-proof dish. Mix together the walnuts and cherries, and spoon the mixture into the centre of each pear half.

Whisk the egg whites until stiff, then fold in the caster sugar. Spoon the meringue mixture over the pears. Cook in the oven at 180°C (350°F) mark 4 for 10 minutes until the meringue is crisp and lightly browned.

Serves 4   110 Calories (460 kJ)
□△   *per portion*

Pineapple salad

A colourful entertaining dessert to serve after a rich dinner party main course.

1 medium pineapple
2 oranges
2 eating apples, cored and diced
30 ml (2 tbsp) dry sherry

Halve the pineapple lengthways. With a sharp knife, scoop out the flesh, cut into cubes, and place in a bowl. Reserve the pine-apple shell. Peel the oranges, removing all the white pith. Cut out the orange segments from the dividing membrane. Add the apple and orange segments to the pineapple cubes. Sprinkle over the sherry and toss together. Divide the fruit between the pineapple shells and chill well before serving.

Serves 4–6   80–115 Calories
□△△   *(325–490 kJ) per portion*

Tangerine melon mousse

Choose a Honeydew, Ogen or Charentais melon to make this delicately-flavoured dessert.

225 g (8 oz) tangerines
225 g (8 oz) melon flesh
10 ml (2 level tsp) powdered gelatine
25 g (1 oz) low-fat skimmed milk powder
1 egg white
liquid artificial sweetener to taste

Grate the tangerine rind without any pith. Remove the peel and neatly chop half the flesh. Chop half the melon. Put 30 ml (2 tbsp) water in a cup and place in a pan of hot water. Sprinkle the gelatine into the cup and heat very gently until dissolved. Put the rest of the fruit, dissolved gelatine, grated tangerine rind, skimmed milk powder and 45 ml (3 tbsp) cold water in a blender and liquidise until smooth.

Transfer to a bowl and, when beginning to thicken, whisk the egg white until thick and carefully fold into the mixture. Add artificial sweetener to taste. Spoon into four glasses and chill. Decorate each one with the reserved chopped tangerine and melon before serving.

Serves 4   55 Calories (225 kJ)
□△   *per portion*

Home-made yogurt

When making your own yogurt, it is not necessary to invest in a commercial yogurt-making machine; a wide-necked insulated jar and a thermometer are the only essentials. Use either low-fat skimmed milk, pasteurised milk or UHT. (UHT is already sterilised so it is the most convenient to use and results in a thick mixture. It does not have to be boiled; just heated to the correct temperature.)

---

568 ml (1 pint) milk (see above)

30 ml (2 tbsp) bought natural yogurt

15 ml (1 level tbsp) skimmed milk powder (optional)

Use absolutely clean, well-rinsed containers and utensils. Warm an insulated jar. Pour the milk into a pan and bring to the boil. Remove from the heat and let the milk cool to 45°C (113°F). Spoon the natural yogurt into a bowl and stir in a little of the cooled milk. Add the skimmed milk powder, if used, to make a smooth paste. Stir in the remaining milk and pour the mixture into the warmed insulated jar. Replace the lid and leave for 6–8 hours, undisturbed. Refrigerate the yogurt as soon as it is ready. When cold, spoon into small containers to serve.

Makes about 600 ml (1 pint)

255 Calories (1065 kJ) per recipe (made with skimmed milk and skimmed milk powder)
415 Calories (1735 kJ) per recipe (made with whole milk and skimmed milk powder)

□ *per 150 ml ($\frac{1}{4}$ pint) (with skimmed milk)*
■ *per 150 ml ($\frac{1}{4}$ pint) (with whole milk)*

VARIATIONS
To sweeten natural yogurt, add honey or artificial sweetener to taste. To flavour, stir in stewed or fresh fruits.

Orange bramble mousse

A delightful creamy fruit mousse which can also be made using fresh blackberries when they are in season.

---

225 g (8 oz) frozen blackberries, thawed

15 ml (1 level tbsp) custard powder

30 ml (2 level tbsp) granulated sugar

300 ml ($\frac{1}{2}$ pint) low-fat skimmed milk

75 ml (3 tbsp) concentrated frozen unsweetened orange juice, thawed

15 ml (3 level tsp) powdered gelatine

3 egg whites

toasted flaked almonds to decorate

Press the blackberries through a sieve, or liquidise in a blender, then sieve. Mix the custard powder and sugar with a little of the milk until smooth. Heat the milk in a pan until almost boiling and stir into the custard mixture. Return to the pan and bring to the boil, stirring, until the custard is smooth and thick. Remove from the heat.

Put the orange juice in a cup and place in a pan of hot water. Sprinkle the gelatine into the juice and heat very gently until dissolved. Whisk together the custard, gelatine and blackberry purée and leave until on the point of setting.

Whisk the egg whites together until stiff and beat 30 ml (2 tbsp) into the blackberry mixture. Carefully fold in the remainder. The first addition of egg white lightens the mixture, allowing the rest to be folded in easily. Spoon into individual glasses and chill. Decorate each glass with flaked almonds just before serving.

Serves 4–6   80–120 Calories
□△   *(335–500 kJ) per portion*

Banana crush

Bananas deteriorate rather quickly so do not buy them too long in advance unless they are fairly green-skinned.

2 eggs
150 ml ($\frac{1}{4}$ pint) low-fat skimmed milk
4 large bananas
juice of 1 lemon
15 g ($\frac{1}{2}$ oz) flaked almonds, toasted

Beat the eggs into the milk and strain into the top of a double saucepan (or bowl placed over a pan of hot water). Heat gently, stirring until thickened. Cool slightly.

Pour the custard into a blender with the peeled and sliced bananas and lemon juice. Liquidise until smooth and divide between four glass dishes. Chill well and sprinkle each glass with nuts just before serving. Use on day of making.

Serves 4   175 Calories (730 kJ)
□△△   per portion

Raspberry sorbet

Always thaw sorbets a little in the refrigerator before serving to bring out the flavour.

225 g (8 oz) fresh or frozen raspberries
300 ml ($\frac{1}{2}$ pint) natural yogurt
15 ml (1 tbsp) lemon juice
10 ml (2 level tsp) powdered gelatine
30 ml (2 level tbsp) caster sugar
2 egg whites

Press the fresh or half-thawed raspberries through a sieve. Combine with the yogurt

and lemon juice. Put 30 ml (2 tbsp) water in a cup and place it in a pan of hot water. Sprinkle the gelatine into the cup and heat gently until dissolved. Add the dissolved gelatine and the sugar to the raspberry mixture.

Stiffly whisk the egg whites and gently fold into the mixture with a metal spoon. Pour into a shallow freezing container or ice tray and freeze.

Serves 4   95 Calories (400 kJ)
□△△   per portion

Baked apple surprise

Serve these unusual baked apples with a spoonful of natural yogurt. Try adding 25 g (1 oz) dried fruit, eg. raisins, dates or sultanas, to the banana filling.

2 medium bananas
15 ml (1 tbsp) lemon juice
1.25 ml ($\frac{1}{4}$ level tsp) grated nutmeg
liquid artificial sweetener to taste
6 medium cooking apples, cored
150 ml ($\frac{1}{4}$ pint) unsweetened orange juice

Peel the bananas and mash with a fork. Mix in the lemon juice and nutmeg. Add artificial sweetener to taste. Make a shallow cut through the skin round the middle of each apple and place in a large baking dish. Fill the centres with the banana mixture and pour the orange juice over them. Bake in the oven at 190°C (375°F) mark 5 for 1 hour until tender, basting occasionally with the orange juice. Cool slightly and serve warm, or chill and serve cold, topped with the remaining orange sauce from the baking dish.

Serves 6   100 Calories (410 kJ)
□△   per portion

Baked custard

Serve with fresh or stewed fruit.

450 ml ($\frac{3}{4}$ pint) low-fat skimmed milk
2 eggs, lightly beaten
liquid artificial sweetener
1.25 ml ($\frac{1}{4}$ tsp) vanilla flavouring
1.25 ml ($\frac{1}{4}$ level tsp) grated nutmeg

Heat the milk until almost boiling and add it to the eggs with a little artificial sweetener and the vanilla flavouring. Stir to combine thoroughly. Pour the mixture into four individual ovenproof dishes and sprinkle with nutmeg. Place in a roasting tin with enough hot water to come halfway up the sides of the dishes. Bake in the oven at 180°C (350°F) mark 4 for 30–45 minutes until firm. Turn out, and serve hot or cold.

Serves 4   80 Calories (345 kJ)
□△   per portion

Ginger fruit salad

A topping of natural yogurt would make a nice addition to this unusual fruit salad.

2 eating apples, cored
2 apricots, skinned and stoned
1 orange, peeled and segmented
241-ml ($8\frac{1}{2}$-fl oz) bottle low-calorie ginger ale
2 bananas
30 ml (2 tbsp) lemon juice
50 g (2 oz) white grapes, seeded

Dice the apples and apricots and put them in a serving bowl with the orange segments and ginger ale. Stir lightly, then leave to marinate for 1 hour.

Peel and slice the bananas and mix them with the lemon juice and grapes. Add them to the marinated fruits. Serve in four individual glasses.

Serves 4   95 Calories (400 kJ)
□△△   per portion

Pear and almond ring

2 eggs
25 g (1 oz) caster sugar
25 g (1 oz) plain flour
10 ml (2 level tsp) cocoa powder
2 large ripe dessert pears, peeled, cored and sliced
60 ml (4 tbsp) unsweetened orange juice
25 g (1 oz) flaked almonds, toasted

Grease and flour a 600-ml (1-pint) plain ring mould. Put the eggs and sugar in a bowl, place over a pan of hot water and whisk until pale and thick. Remove from the heat and continue whisking until cool. Sift the flour and cocoa powder on to the mixture and gently fold in with a metal spoon. Spoon into the prepared tin. Bake in the oven at 190°C (375°F) mark 5 for about 20 minutes until firm to the touch.

Meanwhile, place the pear slices in a pan with the orange juice and cook until just tender. Reserve about half the pear slices and mash the rest with the juices in the pan. Stir in the almonds, return the pear slices to the pan and reheat. Serve quarters of warm sponge with the pear compôte.

Serves 4   170 Calories (720 kJ)
■△   per portion

Grape jelly

An attractive, delicately-flavoured dessert.

150 ml ($\frac{1}{4}$ pint) water
15 ml (3 level tsp) powdered gelatine
few drops green food colouring
450 ml ($\frac{3}{4}$ pint) unsweetened grape juice
225 g (8 oz) white grapes, seeded and skinned
225 g (8 oz) cottage cheese
300 ml ($\frac{1}{2}$ pint) natural yogurt

Put the water in a bowl and place in a pan of hot water. Sprinkle the gelatine over the water and leave to dissolve. Add a few drops of colouring to the grape juice and add to the gelatine. Pour into six glasses. Divide the grapes between the glasses and leave in a cool place to set.

Blend or sieve the cottage cheese until smooth. Fold in the yogurt and top up the glasses. Chill.

Serves 6   110 Calories (455 kJ)
□△   per portion

Baked apples

A popular family dessert with nutritious filling variations to suit everyone's taste. Serve each with a spoonful of natural yogurt, if liked.

4 medium cooking apples
100 g (4 oz) demerara sugar
25 g (1 oz) butter

Make a shallow cut through the skin round the middle of each apple. Core the apples, stand them in an ovenproof dish and pour 60 ml (4 tbsp) water round them. Fill each apple with 25 g (1 oz) sugar and top with a small knob of butter. Bake in the oven at 200°C (400°F) mark 6 for 45 minutes–1 hour until the apples are soft.

ALTERNATIVE FILLINGS
Stuff each apple with 15 ml (1 level tbsp) mincemeat instead of demerara sugar, or with 25 g (1 oz) currants, sultanas, seedless raisins, chopped dried apricots, mixed peel or glacé fruits.

Serves 4   225 Calories (940 kJ)
□△   per portion

Citrus fruit salad

A tangy fruit salad full of vitamin C to serve after a hearty main course.

3 grapefruit
4 oranges
4 tangerines, peeled, or a 312-g (11-oz) can mandarin oranges in natural juice, drained
grated rind of 1 lemon
unsweetened orange juice (see method)

Hold the fruit over a bowl to catch any juice and, with a sharp serrated knife, peel the grapefruit and oranges. Remove all the white pith. Cut the fruit into segments by cutting down the sides of the dividing membranes and cut the segments in half.

Mix the fruit and collected juice in a bowl, together with the tangerine or mandarin orange segments, lemon rind and enough orange juice to moisten. (If canned mandarins are used, there is no need to include the unsweetened orange juice.)

Serves 4   90 Calories (380 kJ)
□△△   per portion

CHAPTER EIGHT

ENTERTAINING

Coq au vin

This popular chicken dish is best served with crusty French bread and fresh green beans. Start the meal with something light, such as Prawn and orange cocktail (see page 55) and finish with a fresh fruit salad.

50 g (2 oz) lean bacon, chopped
100 g (4 oz) mushrooms, sliced
12 button onions, skinned (or 3 medium onions, skinned and sliced)
3 chicken joints, skinned
15 ml (1 level tbsp) cornflour
300 ml ($\frac{1}{2}$ pint) red wine
pinch of grated nutmeg
salt and freshly ground pepper
bouquet garni

Place half the bacon, mushrooms and onions in a 1.7-litre (3-pint) casserole. Arrange the chicken joints on the bed of vegetables and cover with the remaining bacon, mushrooms and onions. Blend the cornflour with a little of the wine, then add the remainder and bring to the boil. Add the nutmeg, salt, pepper and bouquet garni and pour over the chicken. Cook in the oven at 180°C (350°F) mark 4 for about 1–1$\frac{1}{2}$ hours until the chicken is tender. Remove the bouquet garni before serving.

Serves 3   420 Calories (1765 kJ)
■△   *per portion*

Roast stuffed breast of veal

For a large dinner party, a roast is often the easiest thing to cook and this roast stuffed veal makes a change from a plain roast. Serve it with Courgettes and tomatoes au gratin (see page 98) and baked jacket potatoes. Serve grapefruit to start, and finish with a light and refreshing dessert such as Grape jelly (see page 126).

1.6-kg (3$\frac{1}{2}$-lb) boned lean breast of veal, trimmed
grated rind and juice of 1 lemon
2 227-g (8-oz) packets frozen chopped spinach, thawed
1 onion, skinned and finely chopped
5 ml (1 level tsp) grated nutmeg
salt and freshly ground pepper

Brush the veal with the lemon rind and juice. Combine the spinach, onion, nutmeg and salt and pepper. Spread the spinach mixture over the veal, then roll up and tie neatly with string. Brush again with lemon and season well.

Place on a piece of foil large enough to enclose the veal and wrap. Cook in the oven at 190°C (375°F) mark 5 for 2 hours. Unfold the foil and cook for a further 1 hour until brown and the juices run clear when tested with a sharp knife. Serve carved into slices and arranged on a heated serving plate.

Serves 6   240 Calories (1005 kJ)
■△△   *per portion*

Ham steaks Véronique

The combination of cider and grapes makes this ham dish into something special. It needs only Lemony peas and celery (see page 104) to accompany it. Serve a vegetable soup, such as Leek and carrot (see page 51) as a starter, and a light dessert, such as Orange bramble mousse (see page 123) to finish.

6 100-g (4-oz) ham steaks, trimmed

150 ml ($\frac{1}{4}$ pint) cider

150 ml ($\frac{1}{4}$ pint) low-fat skimmed milk

15 g ($\frac{1}{2}$ oz) butter

15 g ($\frac{1}{2}$ oz) flour

salt and freshly ground pepper

175 g (6 oz) white grapes, peeled and seeded

Place the ham steaks slightly overlapping each other in a casserole and pour the cider over. Cook, uncovered, in the oven at 200°C (400°F) mark 6 for 40 minutes, turning once, until tender.

Remove the ham from the casserole and combine the milk with the cider juices from the ham steaks. Keep the ham warm on a heated serving dish.

Melt the butter in a saucepan, add the flour and cook for 1–2 minutes, stirring. Remove from the heat and gradually stir in the cider and milk liquid. Adjust the seasoning, bring to the boil and simmer for 10 minutes, stirring until the sauce is smooth and thick. Add the grapes and heat the sauce through. Pour the sauce over the ham and serve immediately.

Serves 6   225 Calories (940 kJ)
■△   *per portion*

Poached plaice in vermouth

As this special fish dish includes potato, it only needs a fresh green vegetable, such as courgettes or peas, to accompany it. Serve Chicken liver pâté (see page 52) as a starter and Apricot cheesecake (see page 121) for dessert. This would make an ideal meal for a summer lunch-time.

450 g (1 lb) potatoes, peeled

salt and white pepper

75 g (3 oz) butter or margarine

30 ml (2 tbsp) milk

175 g (6 oz) carrots, peeled and finely diced

3 sticks of celery, finely diced

12 plaice fillets, skinned

200 ml (7 fl oz) dry white vermouth

juice of $\frac{1}{2}$ a lemon

175 g (6 oz) button mushrooms, sliced

350 g (12 oz) tomatoes, skinned

Cook the potatoes in a pan of boiling salted water for about 20 minutes until tender. Drain and mash with 15 g ($\frac{1}{2}$ oz) of the fat and the milk. Fill a piping bag, fitted with a large star nozzle, with the mixture. Melt 40 g ($1\frac{1}{2}$ oz) of the fat in a deep frying pan and add the diced vegetables. Fold the fillets, skin side inside, and place on top of the vegetables. Spoon the vermouth over and season well. Cover and cook gently for 10 minutes. Melt the remaining fat in a pan, add the lemon juice and cook the mushrooms, covered, for 5 minutes. Cut the tomatoes into eighths and scoop the seeds into a sieve over a bowl. Discard the seeds but reserve the juice. Scatter the mushrooms, tomatoes and juice over the fish and cook, covered, for a further 5 minutes.

Meanwhile, pipe a ring of potato round a flameproof dish and brown under the grill. Drain the fish and vegetables, reserving the cooking juices, and place in the centre of the potato. Boil the cooking juices to thicken and reduce, if necessary, and spoon over the fish and vegetables.

Serves 6   450 Calories (1880 kJ)
■△   *per portion*

Lamb fillet with lemon and garlic

This flavoursome lamb dish is best served only with plain boiled rice or potatoes. Serve Marinated mushrooms (see page 52) as a starter and Oat-topped apples (see page 116) as a dessert.

700 g (1½ lb) lamb fillet, trimmed
grated rind and juice of 1½ lemons
3 small garlic cloves, skinned and crushed
salt and freshly ground pepper
30 ml (2 tbsp) corn oil
25 g (1 oz) butter or margarine
1 medium onion, skinned and chopped
175 ml (6 fl oz) natural yogurt
150 ml (¼ pint) chicken stock
3 pinches of dried basil
parsley sprigs and lemon slices to garnish

Halve the lamb fillets crossways, then split each piece lengthways. Place each piece between sheets of greaseproof paper and beat out thinly with a meat mallet to resemble escalopes. Put the grated lemon rind into a cup, add the garlic and some pepper. Blend together and spread over the meat. Leave for 15 minutes.

Heat the oil and fat and fry the fillets for about 5 minutes on each side. Drain, transfer to a heated serving dish and keep warm. Pour off all but 30 ml (2 tbsp) fat from the pan and lightly brown the onion. Stir in the yogurt, stock, lemon juice and basil, bring to the boil and simmer for 2–3 minutes. Adjust the seasoning. Spoon the juices over the meat and garnish with parsley and lemon.

Serves 4   400 Calories (1670 kJ)
■△   per portion

Poulet chasseur

Grapefruit and orange cocktail (see page 55) would make a refreshing starter to serve before this dish, which could be accompanied by plain boiled vegetables, such as new potatoes and courgettes. Serve Walnut pear meringue (see page 122) for dessert.

1–2 carrots, peeled and chopped
½ turnip, peeled and chopped
½ swede, peeled and chopped
1 small onion, skinned and chopped
1 stick of celery, chopped
4 chicken joints, skinned
450 ml (¾ pint) chicken stock
2 tomatoes, roughly chopped
salt and freshly ground pepper
15 ml (1 tbsp) sherry

To garnish

100 g (4 oz) mushrooms, grilled
8 lean bacon rashers, rolled and grilled

Place the vegetables in a large saucepan and arrange the chicken joints on top. Add the stock, tomatoes and salt and pepper. Bring to the boil, then simmer gently for 1–1½ hours until tender.

Remove the chicken and strain the sauce, keeping the vegetables and chicken hot. Thicken the liquor by boiling rapidly to reduce by about half. Add the sherry and season to taste. Mound the vegetables in a heated serving dish and place the chicken portions on top. Pour a little sauce over and garnish with grilled mushrooms and bacon rolls. Serve the remaining sauce separately.

Serves 4   280 Calories (1170 kJ)
■△△   per portion

Lamb bourguignonne

Serve Grapefruit, apple and mint cocktail (see page 54) to start and Pineapple salad (see page 122) as a dessert. The lamb dish needs only simple accompaniments, such as boiled new potatoes and a green salad.

1.1 kg (2½ lb) lean leg of lamb (boned weight), trimmed
225 g (8 oz) button onions, skinned
225 g (8 oz) button mushrooms
250 ml (8 fl oz) red wine
300 ml (½ pint) beef stock
salt and freshly ground pepper
15 ml (1 level tbsp) arrowroot
chopped fresh parsley and toasted croûtons to garnish

Cut the lamb into bite-size pieces. Place the meat and onions in a pan and add the mushrooms. Pour over the wine, stock and salt and pepper. Bring to the boil, cover tightly and simmer for about 50 minutes until the lamb is tender. Blend the arrowroot with a little water, stir into the juices and cook for about 2 minutes until clear. Serve garnished with parsley and croûtons.

Serves 6   300 Calories (1250 kJ)
■△   *per portion*

Apple and lemon lamb

This would be ideal for a summer lunchtime, served with boiled fresh courgettes and rice. Fresh fruit and a selection of cheeses would round off the meal nicely.

450 g (1 lb) lean leg or fillet of lamb, trimmed
1 lemon, thinly sliced
5 ml (1 level tsp) dried thyme
salt and freshly ground pepper
150 ml (¼ pint) chicken stock
1 eating apple, cored and sliced
parsley sprigs to garnish

Cut the lamb into 5-cm (2-inch) strips. Place in a shallow flameproof casserole and cover with the lemon slices. Stir the thyme, salt and pepper into the stock and pour over the lamb. Bring to the boil and simmer for 30 minutes.

Arrange the apple slices over the lemon and cook for a further 15 minutes until the lamb, apple and lemon are tender. Serve garnished with parsley.

Serves 4   230 Calories (960 kJ)
■△   *per portion*

Grilled cutlets with gooseberry sauce

An unusual combination of flavours, this dish is ideal for entertaining. Serve Mushroom bouillon (see page 46) as a starter and finish the meal with a selection of cheeses and fresh fruit.

8 small lamb cutlets, trimmed
salt and freshly ground pepper
225 g (8 oz) gooseberries, topped and tailed
7 g ($\frac{1}{4}$ oz) butter
liquid artificial sweetener to taste
pinch of grated nutmeg
watercress sprigs to garnish

Sprinkle the cutlets with salt and pepper. Place under a hot grill and cook for 2–3 minutes on each side until lightly browned. Reduce the heat and continue cooking until the cutlets are cooked through. Transfer to a heated serving dish and keep hot.

To make the sauce, put the gooseberries in a pan with a very little water and simmer gently until soft and mushy—there should be no water remaining. Press the gooseberries through a sieve and add the butter, artificial sweetener and nutmeg to taste. Serve with grilled tomatoes and garnish with sprigs of watercress.

Serves 4   225 Calories (935 kJ)
■△   per portion

Lamb tikka kebabs

Watercress soup (see page 48 and double the recipe) could be served as a starter, and Florida sponge pudding (see page 117) as a dessert. This dish must be prepared two days ahead to allow the spices to mellow. Serve simply with a fresh green salad and plain boiled white or brown rice. Garam masala is a mixture of spices available from most grocery shops.

450 g (1 lb) lean lamb fillet, cubed
8–12 button onions, skinned
1 small green pepper, seeded
175 g (6 oz) button mushrooms
lemon wedges to garnish

For the marinade

150 ml ($\frac{1}{4}$ pint) natural yogurt
5 ml (1 level tsp) garam masala
5 ml (1 level tsp) ground cumin seed
1.25 ml ($\frac{1}{4}$ level tsp) ground coriander
1.25 ml ($\frac{1}{4}$ level tsp) ground turmeric
1.25 ml ($\frac{1}{4}$ level tsp) grated nutmeg
2.5 ml ($\frac{1}{2}$ level tsp) garlic powder
2.5 ml ($\frac{1}{2}$ level tsp) chilli seasoning
juice and finely grated rind of 1 lemon

Combine the ingredients for the marinade in a large bowl. Add the lamb and turn to coat evenly. Leave to marinate in the refrigerator for two days, stirring occasionally.

Before starting to cook, simmer the onions in water for 10 minutes (or use well-drained cocktail onions). Cut the pepper into 2.5-cm (1-inch) squares and blanch for 2 minutes in boiling water, then drain well. Remove the lamb from the marinade. Thread the lamb, mushrooms, onions and pepper alternately on to flat skewers and place on a baking sheet. Place under a moderate grill for 15–20 minutes or until the meat is cooked. Garnish with lemon wedges. Serve the kebabs on the skewers arranged on a bed of rice.

Serves 4   200 Calories (840 kJ)
■△   per portion

Chicken Marengo

For an informal dinner party, serve Cream of celery soup (see page 48), followed by Chicken Marengo with broccoli spears and baked jacket potatoes. Finish the meal with Date-filled oranges (see page 114).

1.4-kg (3-lb) chicken, jointed and skinned
100 g (4 oz) carrots, peeled and sliced
100 g (4 oz) mushrooms, sliced
1 medium onion, skinned and chopped
450 ml ($\frac{3}{4}$ pint) hot chicken stock
salt and freshly ground pepper
15 ml (1 tbsp) white wine

Place the chicken joints in a flameproof casserole. Add the carrots, mushrooms and onion, pour over the stock and add salt and pepper. Cover and bake in the oven at 180°C (350°F) mark 4 for 1½ hours until tender.

Place the chicken on a heated serving dish and keep warm. Add the wine to the liquid, boil rapidly to thicken and reduce, then pour over the chicken.

Serves 4   240 Calories (1000 kJ)
■△   *per portion*

Marinated steak

For a special occasion, serve Cod's roe pâté (see page 53), followed by this steak dish with plain boiled rice or new potatoes and a mixed salad. As the first two courses are quite filling, you'll need no more than a fresh fruit salad for dessert.

1 garlic clove, skinned and crushed
30 ml (2 tbsp) corn oil
120 ml (8 tbsp) red wine
15 ml (1 level tbsp) tomato purée
350 g (12 oz) rump steak, trimmed
watercress sprigs to garnish

Combine the garlic, oil, wine and tomato purée, and place with the steak in a polythene bag. Leave for 4–5 hours in a cool place.

Drain the steak, reserving the marinade, and cook under a medium grill for 5–7 minutes on each side (depending on thickness). Boil the marinade rapidly until reduced to about 30 ml (2 tbsp), and serve as a sauce. Serve garnished with watercress.

Serves 2   370 Calories (1500 kJ)
■△   *per portion*

Whiting korma

Serve this spicy fish dish with 100 g (4 oz) plain or brown boiled rice and a salad of 225 g (8 oz) sliced tomatoes and 1 small bunch of watercress in 30 ml (2 tbsp) oil and vinegar dressing. Finish the meal with refreshing bowls of chilled fresh fruit salad.

150 ml ($\frac{1}{4}$ pint) natural yogurt
5 ml (1 level tsp) curry paste
1.25 ml ($\frac{1}{4}$ level tsp) ground coriander
1.25 ml ($\frac{1}{4}$ level tsp) ground ginger
1.25 ml ($\frac{1}{4}$ level tsp) ground turmeric
pinch of salt
450 g (1 lb) whiting fillets

Combine the yogurt with the curry paste, coriander, ginger, turmeric and salt. Place the unskinned fillets in the marinade, spreading it evenly over the fish, and leave for 2–3 hours.

Arrange the fish with the marinade in a small baking dish. Cook in the oven at 180°C (350°F) mark 4 for about 20 minutes until tender.

Serves 2   220 Calories (910 kJ)
□△   *per portion*

French veal cutlets

Serve Red pepper soup (see page 51) as a starter and Green beans Sorrento (see page 107) and boiled new potatoes with the veal cutlets. Finish with Coconut fruit crisp (see page 114).

700 g (1$\frac{1}{2}$ lb) best end of neck of veal or 4 cutlets, trimmed
100 g (4 oz) lean bacon, chopped
10 shallots, skinned and chopped
1 garlic clove, skinned and crushed
chervil sprig
salt and freshly ground pepper

If the meat is in one piece, divide it into four cutlets. Gently heat the bacon until the fat runs and fry the shallots, garlic and chervil for 5–7 minutes. Season well. Place the cutlets under a hot grill and cook on both sides for about 10 minutes until tender. Arrange on a heated serving dish and place a spoonful of the shallot mixture on each.

Serves 4   265 Calories (1110 kJ)
■△   *per portion*

Paella

Illustrated in colour on page 120

This makes an ideal dish for an informal supper party, served with just a green salad. If you want to serve a starter, chilled melon would be perfect as it needs very little preparation. A selection of cheeses and fresh fruit is all that's needed to finish off the meal.

350 g (12 oz) chicken breast, skinned
75 g (3 oz) onion, skinned and sliced
1 garlic clove, skinned and crushed
450 ml ($\frac{3}{4}$ pint) chicken stock
225 g (8 oz) long-grain rice
100 g (4 oz) red pepper, seeded and sliced
2.5 ml ($\frac{1}{2}$ level tsp) ground turmeric
salt and freshly ground pepper
100 g (4 oz) tomatoes, quartered
100 g (4 oz) shelled prawns
100 g (4 oz) frozen French beans
600 ml (1 pint) mussels in the shell, scrubbed

Cut the chicken into bite-size pieces. Place in a pan with the onion, garlic and stock. Bring to the boil and add the rice, red pepper, turmeric and salt and pepper. Simmer gently, uncovered, for 20 minutes. Add the tomatoes, prawns and beans and continue to cook until all the moisture is absorbed.

Meanwhile, cook the prepared mussels in 1 cm ($\frac{1}{2}$ inch) of salted water for 5 minutes. Discard any mussels that do not open. Remove all but four mussels from the shells and add to the paella. Place the mussels in their shells upside-down on the paella to reheat for a few minutes, then turn them right side up to garnish. Serve immediately.

Serves 4   300 Calories (1250 kJ)
□△   *per portion*

Turkey supremes en papillote

Serve with a mixed salad and boiled potatoes. For a complete menu, Spinach soup (see page 51) would make a nice starter, and Rhubarb and almond compote (see page 121) is a delicious dessert.

550–700 g (1$\frac{1}{4}$–1$\frac{1}{2}$ lb) turkey breasts, skinned and boned
15 ml (1 tbsp) corn oil
1 small red pepper, seeded and finely sliced
225 g (8 oz) tomatoes, skinned and sliced
30 ml (2 tbsp) chopped fresh parsley
salt and freshly ground pepper
60 ml (4 tbsp) medium dry sherry
40 g (1$\frac{1}{2}$ oz) fresh white breadcrumbs, toasted

Split each turkey breast, place between sheets of greaseproof paper and beat with a meat mallet until thin. Line a baking sheet with oiled foil. Put half the turkey breasts side by side on it. Blanch the red pepper in boiling water for 2 minutes, then drain. Layer the pepper, tomatoes, half the parsley and seasoning on top of the turkey. Cover with the rest of the turkey. Spoon over the sherry and wrap in the foil. Cook in the oven at 180°C (350°F) mark 4 for 35–40 minutes until the pepper, tomatoes and turkey are tender.

Arrange the turkey supremes on a heated serving dish and keep warm. Boil the juices rapidly to reduce to 60 ml (4 tbsp) and spoon over the meat. Sprinkle with the breadcrumbs and garnish with the remaining parsley.

Serves 4   265 Calories (1100 kJ)
□△   *per portion*

Southern beef and bean pot

Complement the unusual combination of flavours in this dish with Dressed French beans (see page 108) and boiled new potatoes. Serve Chicken liver pâté (see page 52) as a starter and Frozen summer fruit sundae (see page 118) to complete the meal.

---

100 g (4 oz) rose cocoa beans, soaked overnight

---

1 kg (2 lb) lean chuck steak, trimmed

---

2 medium onions, skinned and sliced

---

450 ml ($\frac{3}{4}$ pint) beef stock

---

1 bay leaf

---

8 juniper berries

---

thinly pared rind of $\frac{1}{2}$ an orange

---

salt and freshly ground pepper

---

chopped fresh parsley to garnish

Drain the beans well. Cut the meat into bite-size pieces and place in a flameproof casserole or saucepan. Add the onion, stock, beans, bay leaf, berries, orange rind and salt and pepper. Bring to the boil, cover and simmer for about 2 hours, stirring from time to time. Discard the orange rind and bay leaf and serve garnished with parsley.

Serves 6   300 Calories (1250 kJ)
■△△   *per portion*

Tropical chicken

The luxury of peaches makes this chicken casserole an ideal dinner party dish. Start the meal with Leek and carrot soup (see page 51), serve Tomato and onion bake (see page 107) and rice with the chicken, and complete the meal with cheese and fresh fruit.

---

6 175-g (6-oz) chicken breasts, skinned

2.5 ml ($\frac{1}{2}$ level tsp) paprika

411-g ($14\frac{1}{2}$-oz) can peach slices in natural juice

180-g ($6\frac{1}{4}$-oz) frozen concentrated unsweetened orange juice, thawed

---

15 ml (1 tbsp) vinegar

---

salt and freshly ground pepper

Dust the chicken with paprika and press in gently. Place in a casserole large enough to take the chicken in a single layer.

Drain the peaches well and pat dry on absorbent kitchen paper. Arrange between the chicken. Combine the orange juice, vinegar and salt and pepper and spoon over the chicken. Cover and cook in the oven at 190°C (375°F) mark 5 for about 1 hour, basting the chicken twice with the juices during cooking, until the chicken is tender. Drain off the juices and reduce to a glaze by boiling rapidly. Spoon over the chicken.

Serves 6   200 Calories (840 kJ)
□△   *per portion*

Moussaka

Moussaka is a traditional Greek dish. Serve Cod's roe pâté (see page 53 and double the recipe) as a starter and Date-filled oranges (see page 114) as a dessert. Moussaka needs little accompaniment—just French bread and a salad. To be sure the meat is lean, mince it yourself.

2 medium aubergines, sliced
salt and freshly ground pepper
450 g (1 lb) lean minced beef or lamb
45 ml (3 level tbsp) tomato purée
3 onions, skinned and sliced
4 tomatoes, sliced
15 ml (1 tbsp) corn oil
150 ml (¼ pint) natural yogurt
15 ml (1 level tbsp) grated Parmesan cheese

Sprinkle the aubergine slices with salt and leave for 30 minutes. Rinse well and dry on absorbent kitchen paper.

Place about half of the aubergine slices in a casserole. Fry the beef for 5 minutes until brown. Strain off the excess fat and season. Add the tomato purée and onions. Place half the mince mixture over the aubergines in the casserole. Add a layer of half the tomatoes, then more mince and finally the remaining tomatoes. Top with the rest of the aubergines and brush with the oil. Cover and cook in the oven at 180°C (350°F) mark 4 for about 1 hour until the meat and aubergines are tender.

Spread the yogurt over the aubergines and sprinkle on the cheese. Place under a moderate grill for a few minutes to brown before serving.

Serves 4   265 Calories (1110 kJ)
■△△   *per portion*

Mexican chicken

Serve this unusual, flavoursome chicken casserole with plain boiled vegetables, such as French beans and new potatoes. Lettuce and cucumber soup (see page 46) would be a suitable starter with creamy Banana and hazelnut fool (see page 115) for dessert.

225 g (8 oz) aubergine, skinned and sliced
salt and freshly ground pepper
4 175-g (6-oz) chicken portions, skinned
175 g (6 oz) onion, skinned and chopped
226-g (8-oz) can tomatoes
15 ml (1 tbsp) vinegar
10 ml (2 level tsp) demerara sugar
10 ml (2 level tsp) mustard powder
30 ml (2 tbsp) Worcestershire sauce
pinch of chilli powder

Sprinkle the aubergine slices with salt and leave for 30 minutes. Rinse well and dry on absorbent kitchen paper. Place the chicken portions in a casserole. Place the aubergines, onion, tomatoes, vinegar, sugar, mustard, Worcestershire sauce and seasonings in a pan and bring to the boil. Pour over the chicken. Cook in the oven at 190°C (375°F) mark 5 for 1–1½ hours until the chicken is tender.

Serves 4   180 Calories (755 kJ)
■△   *per portion*

Baked mullet stuffed with mushrooms

On a warm summer's evening, serve Iced cucumber soup (see page 46 and halve the recipe) as a starter, and follow the Baked mullet with a fresh fruit salad made from delicious soft summer fruits. Serve boiled new potatoes and Dressed broccoli (see page 105) with the Baked mullet.

2 whole 225-g (8-oz) red mullet, cleaned
50 g (2 oz) mushrooms, sliced
60 ml (4 tbsp) red wine
salt and freshly ground pepper
6 anchovy fillets
2 large tomatoes, skinned and chopped

Place the mullet on two 25.5-cm (10-inch) squares of foil. Gently cook the mushrooms in a pan with the wine and season well. Spoon into the cavity of the fish. Slash the skin of each fish two or three times.

Snip the anchovies into small pieces and tuck into the slashes. Top with the tomatoes and season with pepper. Wrap the fish in the foil and place on a baking sheet. Bake in the oven at 190°C (375°F) mark 5 for about 20 minutes.

Serves 2   295 Calories (1235 kJ)
□△   *per portion*

Tandoori poussin

For a winter dinner party, serve Mushroom bouillon (see page 46) as a starter, and a citrus fruit salad dessert. Serve the Tandoori poussin with rice and Cucumber salad (see page 99).

2 1-kg (2-lb) poussins
25 ml (5 level tsp) tandoori mixture
300 ml (½ pint) natural yogurt
juice of 2 small lemons
pinch of salt
30 ml (2 tbsp) corn oil
chopped fresh parsley to garnish

Skin and halve each poussin, removing the backbone using kitchen scissors. Combine the tandoori mixture with the yogurt, lemon juice and salt. Pour over the poussins, cover and leave in the refrigerator overnight.

Remove the poussins from the marinade, brush with a little oil and place under a moderate grill for about 10 minutes until golden. Place in an ovenproof dish and pour over the marinade. Cover and cook in the oven at 180°C (350°F) mark 4 for 30–40 minutes, basting occasionally. Pour the juices from the dish, skim off the fat and boil rapidly in a pan to reduce. Spoon the juices over the poussins and garnish with parsley.

Serves 4   410 Calories (1715 kJ)
■△   *per portion*

Beef in wine

These rolled steaks make an unusual dinner party dish. Serve with braised carrots and Dijon potatoes (see page 111). Spinach soup (see page 51) would make a suitable starter. Choose a dessert that can be made in advance, such as Blackberry whip (see page 115).

2 225-g (8-oz) pieces quick-fry steak, trimmed

100 g (4 oz) mushrooms, finely chopped

½ small green pepper, seeded and chopped

4 stuffed olives, sliced

30 ml (2 level tbsp) tomato purée

15 ml (1 tbsp) lemon juice

salt and freshly ground pepper

60 ml (4 tbsp) red wine

Place the steaks between two sheets of grease-proof paper and beat them with a meat mallet until fairly thin. Cut each into two. In a small bowl, mix together the mushrooms, green pepper, olives, tomato purée and lemon juice. Divide the mixture between the four steaks, sprinkle lightly with salt and pepper and roll up each one.

Place each rolled steak in a piece of foil large enough to enclose it. Pour 15 ml (1 tbsp) red wine over each roll and wrap in the foil. Place in a baking tin and cook in the oven at 180°C (350°F) mark 4 for about 30 minutes. Remove from the foil, place on a heated serving plate, and spoon over the juices from the foil parcels.

Serves 4   245 Calories (1030 kJ)
■△   *per portion*

Chicken Chinese

This oriental chicken dish has to be prepared and served very quickly, so serve a starter that needs little preparation, such as chilled melon, and a dessert that can be made in advance, such as Raspberry sorbet (see page 124). The chicken needs only boiled rice as an accompaniment.

4 225-g (8-oz) chicken joints, skinned

30 ml (2 tbsp) corn oil

45 ml (3 tbsp) soy sauce

30 ml (2 level tbsp) tomato purée

1 onion, skinned and sliced

2 medium carrots, peeled and cut into matchsticks

½ green pepper, seeded and finely sliced

100 g (4 oz) mushrooms, sliced

270-g (9½-oz) can beansprouts, drained

283-g (10-oz) can bamboo shoots, drained and finely cut into matchsticks

15 ml (1 tbsp) dry sherry

Cut the flesh from the chicken joints and slice into strips. Heat the oil, add the chicken and quickly fry, stirring continuously for 10–15 minutes until tender. Stir in the soy sauce and tomato purée. Add the onion, carrot and green pepper and fry for 5 minutes, stirring frequently. Add the mushrooms, beansprouts, bamboo shoots and sherry. Heat through, stirring well, then serve.

Serves 4   280 Calories (1170 kJ)
■△△   *per portion*

A schedule of exercises for the family

Fat or fit? Medical research confirms every-day experience: It really isn't possible to be both.

It is generally believed today that being very overweight can increase the risk of contracting such illnesses as heart disease, bronchitis and arthritis, and anyone who has ever been even a little overweight will know how much better it feels to be at the correct weight. They will also know how hard it can be to shed those extra unwanted pounds. This is why it is so important to maintain a healthy balanced diet, as outlined in chapter 1, so that you and your family need never face the problems of being overweight.

Over the last 30 years, magazine articles about obesity, slimming plans and doctors' advice to overweight people have concentrated on low-calorie diets as the only key to healthy weight reduction and the contribution of exercise to a slimming plan has been underestimated. When slimmers are told that they would need to walk from London to Brighton to lose just 500 g (1 lb) of weight, it's no wonder they lose heart and prefer to concentrate on counting calories.

HOW CAN EXERCISE HELP?

We now know that although exercise alone will make little long-term difference to weight, combined with a healthy diet it will speed up both the rate at which the body burns up stored fat, and metabolism — the rate at which the body uses up food. *Regular* exercise can make a dramatic difference to the speed of weight loss. Not only is the rate of metabolism pushed up during exercise, but the body goes on burning up calories for some time after exercising in order to meet the next demand to be made on it.

WHO NEEDS TO EXERCISE?

It's not only the would-be slimmer who should take regular exercise. Every member of the family needs to keep fit in order to cope with sudden or prolonged physical or emotional stress and to avoid a whole range of diseases that are closely related to lack of exercise. Quite simply, health and fitness depend on exercise just as much as on eating the right foods.

Exercise needn't be boring. The most valuable kinds — walking, cycling, swimming, dancing — can be fun and can be enjoyed by the whole family. Children, of course, get most of the exercise they need while playing or during physical education lessons at school, so it isn't so important for them to do regular exercises as well.

Being fit can make a tremendous difference to the way you feel. Even the most sedentary, car-borne worker will find that after a few sessions at the swimming pool, for instance, he's better able to climb stairs without puffing, and can cope with weekend gardening without strain. A regular exercise programme should be the next step on the road to all-round physical fitness.

CAN EXERCISE BE DANGEROUS?

People who are unfit may worry that exercise could be dangerous. Anyone over 40, or with a history of heart disease or joint trouble, or who is at all doubtful, should certainly consult a doctor before embarking on any exercise programme. The schedule of exercises suggested here was developed by Al Murray, Director of the City Gym Health Clinic in London and, *provided they are tackled very gradually to start with*, building up slowly to the full programme, they should be nothing but positive benefit. However, if you feel any pain in the chest, arms, back or joints or develop a headache or feel dizzy while exercising, stop immediately and consult your doctor.

CHECKING YOUR PULSE-RATE

Anyone in doubt about the effect of the exercises on the heart and lungs can check his pulse-rate immediately after a small amount of exercise. Using a watch with a second-hand, measure this over 30 seconds, finding the pulse on the wrist and pressing lightly with the fingers of the other hand (see illustration). Double the resulting count for the pulse-rate per minute. To find your safe rate, add your age in years to an 'unfitness handi-cap' of 40 and subtract the total from 200. Someone of 40 thus subtracts 80 from 200. In this case, 120 is the pulse-rate that should not be exceeded in the early days of the exercise programme. Later, the handicap can be gradually reduced as fitness improves. For young people, it can be reduced to 0, but probably not below 20 for people over 50.

THE EXERCISE SCHEDULE

The exercises illustrated on the next few pages are intended to promote and develop the 3 vital elements of physical fitness— mobility, strength and stamina. For the majority of people who simply want to get and keep fit, working through this schedule will be enough. Aim to work up *gradually* to the speed and frequency indicated for each exercise, exercising for 15–20 minutes 3 times a week. After this target has been reached, anyone aiming at super-fitness can go further. The Health Education Council's free booklet *Look After Yourself* is obtainable from local health authorities or direct from the HEC, 78 New Oxford Street, London WC1A 1AH. It describes Al Murray's pro-gramme in greater detail and illustrates a set of more advanced follow-on exercises for fit people who want to be even fitter.

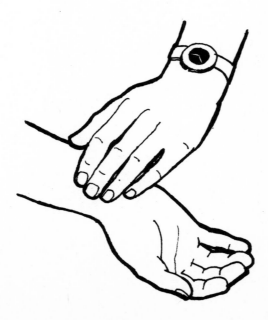

Exercises for mobility (Suppleness)

These should be done at a relaxed tempo, *gradually* increasing the range of mobility, never forcing it. Work up gradually to 12 repetitions of each exercise.

1 ARM SWINGING Stand with feet wide apart, arms loosely by your sides. Raise both arms forwards, upwards, backwards and sideways in a circular movement, brushing the ears with your arms as you go.

2 SIDE BENDS Stand with feet wide apart and hands on hips. Bend left, then right, keeping the head in line with the trunk.

3 TRUNK, KNEE AND HIP BENDS
Stand with feet together about 0.5 m (18 inches) behind the back of a dining or kitchen chair, both hands resting lightly on the chairback. Raise one knee and bring the forehead down to meet it. Repeat with the other knee. Don't hurry—this should be a strong, smooth movement. Later, do this exercise without a chair, slightly bending the knee of the supporting leg.

4 HEAD, ARMS AND TRUNK ROTATING Stand with feet wide apart, arms held forward at shoulder level. Keeping hips and legs still, turn the head, arms and shoulders as far as possible to the left, bending the right arm across the chest. Repeat to the right.

5 ALTERNATE ANKLE REACHING Stand with feet wide apart, palms on front of upper left thigh. Slide both hands down front of leg. Return to upright position and repeat to the right. *If you suffer from mild back trouble do not pass below the knees with the hands.*

Exercises for strength

Start with 8–10 repetitions of each exercise, then work up *gradually* to 20–30 repetitions. Don't go on to the next level until you can do the one you're on easily.

a Stand at arms' length from a wall. Place the hands 30.5 cm (12 inches) apart at shoulder height on the wall. Rise on the toes and bend the arms until chest and chin touch the wall. Straighten arms and return to the original position.

b Stand with hands 30.5 cm (12 inches) apart on a firm table with arms straight and extended. Bend arms, keeping body straight until chest touches table. Return to original position. (Some women may find **c** and **d** too difficult so should only do **a** and **b**.)

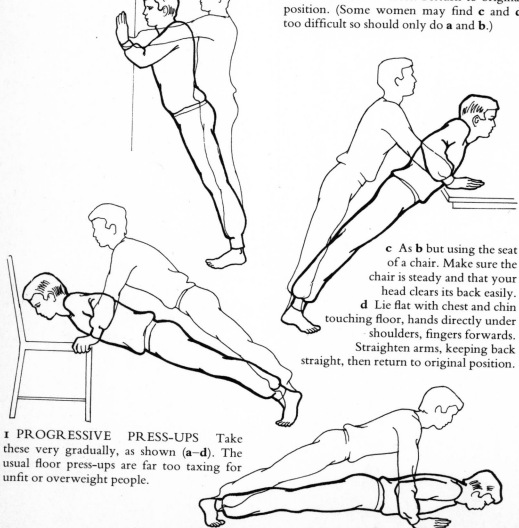

c As **b** but using the seat of a chair. Make sure the chair is steady and that your head clears its back easily.
d Lie flat with chest and chin touching floor, hands directly under shoulders, fingers forwards. Straighten arms, keeping back straight, then return to original position.

1 PROGRESSIVE PRESS-UPS Take these very gradually, as shown (**a–d**). The usual floor press-ups are far too taxing for unfit or overweight people.

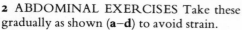

2 ABDOMINAL EXERCISES Take these gradually as shown (**a–d**) to avoid strain.

a Sit forward on chair, legs straight, heels on floor. Lean back, gripping the sides of the seat for support, bending the knees and bringing the fronts of the thighs up to press lightly against the body.

b Same exercise as **a** with legs straight.

c Lie on back, knees slightly bent, feet tucked under low heavy chair or settee. Swing up to sitting position and stretch hands forwards to ankles (no further).

d Lie on back, hands behind head, heels up on edge of chair. Swing up to sitting position, bending the knees slightly.

3 LEG EXERCISES Unfit adults will find these exercises difficult because of weakness in the legs. *Take them gradually* to avoid undue strain. Start with **a**, then progress to **b**, **c** and **d**.

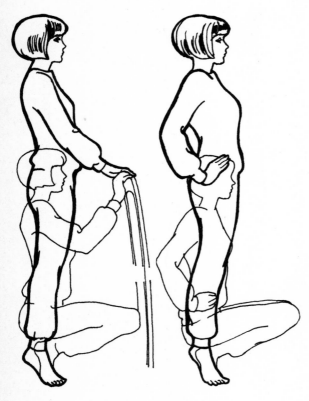

a Stand 0.5 m (18 inches) behind a chair, hands on chair back. Lower the body to squat—men keeping feet flat on floor, women rising to toes. Straighten the legs and come up on toes. Repeat.
b As **a** but without chair and hands on hips.
c As **b**, but come up fast so that you jump in the air—a few inches at first, higher later.
d Start in half-squat (see illustration), then leap upwards into star jump. Relax knees on landing to cushion shock.

Exercises for stamina (Heart and Lungs)

Pulse-taking (see page 141) is the best way to ensure that you are not overdoing these exercises. Take your pulse every minute or so; if it is at or below your 'safe' rate you can continue. If the rate is higher, rest until the pulse comes down. The aim of these stamina-building exercises is to maintain the personal pulse-rate *and no higher* for a period of 10 minutes' continuous exercise. At first, pulse-taking involves frequent stopping and starting. Later, rest periods get shorter and shorter until the full 10 minutes' exercise is achieved.

1 RUNNING ON THE SPOT Stand with arms loosely by your sides. Run gently on the spot for 30 seconds, building up to 5 or 6 minutes. Check pulse-rate frequently. Gradually raise the knees higher as you progress without strain. Move on to exercise **2**.

2 BENCH OR STAIR STEPPING Stand with hands on hips 30.5 cm (12 inches) away from a stair, low stool or sturdy box. Step up on to it 15 times with one foot leading, 15 times with the other. Increase gradually to 30 times with each foot. If possible, increase the height to a maximum of 18 inches. Then aim at 3 to 6 minutes' continuous exercise without exceeding your pulse-rate. Move on to exercise **3**.

3 OUTDOOR EXERCISE Once **2** comes easily, move on to jogging, swimming or cycling, aiming to do 10 minutes continuously. Check your pulse-rate frequently, as before. After a month or more, cautiously raise the pulse rate by steps of 5 beats per minute to a maximum of 20.

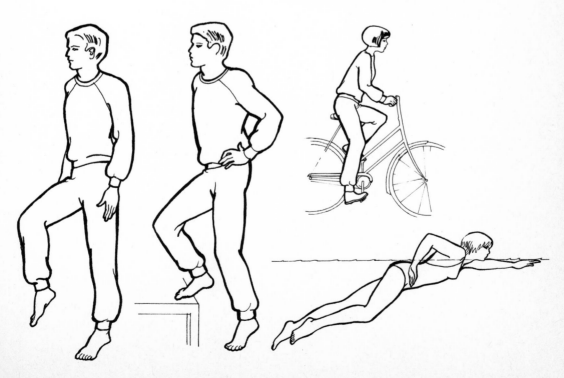

INDEX

INDEX

INDEX